Praise for *When He Opens the Heavens*

"Dr. Alemu Beeftu has an amazing ability to take a profound spiritual truth and make it easy to understand. He *epitomizes* what can occur through a mature blending of Christ's apostolic and teaching anointings. Alemu's personal story *epitomizes* God's grace, mercy, and supernatural ability. And his latest of more than 50 books, *When He Opens the Heavens*, *epitomizes* what a great book should do: change the reader. God wants to open the heavens over your life, home, family, business, city, and nation. This tremendous book will show you how."

—**Dutch Sheets**, Founder and President of Dutch Sheets Ministries and author of *Intercessory Prayer*

"In his new book *When He Opens the Heavens*, Alemu Beeftu gives us a behind-the-scenes look into how God manipulates the heavens over us. It is a revelational, educational, and instructional masterpiece on how to discern the activity of God in our lives. This is a phenomenal book."

—**Isaac Pitre**, II Kings Global Network

"Dr. Alemu Beeftu unlocks much-needed revelation and understanding of the concepts of what Scripture teaches about open heavens in this new book. By weaving wisdom and revelation out of the Scriptures, Dr. Beeftu provides solid Biblical teaching in regard to open heavens as related to people, places, opportunities, processes, purpose, and so much more. This book overflows with deep spiritual wisdom, revelation, knowledge, and understanding that promises to bring greater weight to our prayers and pursuit of God opening the heavens over us in our generation. Keep reading and expect to encounter the God who opens heavens as you do."

—**Jacquie Tyre**, Apostle, City

"In his book *When He Opens the Heavens*, Dr. Alemu Beeftu provides biblical foundation to help us to understand God's desire for humanity to access him. Recommend this book to all who desire not only to live under an open heaven but also to access God's presence in an incredible way."

—**Dr. Venner Alston,**
author of *Next Level Believers* and *Image Bearers*

"Dr. Alemu Beeftu has written a kingdom book for the strange and uncertain times in which we now live. In *When He Opens the Heavens: Responding to God's Invitation with Praise and Purpose*, Alemu lays a clear path for you to build your life and destiny—a blueprint from Father God's heart. As you read, you will find yourself shedding off religious ideologies, philosophies, and bad theology that have held you in bondage. You have not picked up this book by accident. There is a strategy to your journey and your assignment. A solution is at hand. In the pages of this fantastic book, you will discover what you need to fulfill your assignment as a mighty Kingdom advancer. I am honored to endorse this much-needed manuscript. Don't just read this work. Study it! Embrace it! Practice it! Then, get ready for change."

—**Dr. Greg Hood,** ThD,
President, Kingdom University, Apostolic Leader at Network
of Five-Fold Ministers & Churches and Kingdom Life Ekklesia,
Franklin, Tennessee; author of *The Gospel of the Kingdom*

When He
Opens
the
Heavens

Responding to God's Invitation
with Praise and Purpose

Alemu Beeftu, PhD

PARACLETE PRESS
Brewster, Massachusetts

2024 First Printing

When He Opens the Heavens: Responding to God's Invitation with Praise and Purpose

Copyright © 2024 by Alemu Beeftu
ISBN 978-1-64060-895-5

NOTE: In this book you will see words like person, his, him and others. In the Bible these words are gender neutral. I have followed the same pattern. Please keep this in mind.

The Paraclete Press name and logo (dove on cross) are trademarks of Paraclete Press

Library of Congress Cataloging-in-Publication Data
Names: Beeftu, Alemu, author.
Title: When He opens the heavens : responding to God's invitation with praise and purpose / Alemu Beeftu, PhD.
Description: Brewster, Massachusetts : Paraclete Press, [2024] | Summary: "Dr Beeftu offers a deep reflection on biblical narratives that explore open heavens, open doors, open gates, and open hearts to encourage and educate the Body of Christ about prophetic destiny. With new revelation from Scripture, walk with God as He opens the Heavens over your life"-- Provided by publisher.
Identifiers: LCCN 2024004115 (print) | LCCN 2024004116 (ebook) | ISBN 9781640608955 (trade paperback) | ISBN 9781640608979 (pdf) | ISBN 9781640608962 (epub)
Subjects: LCSH: Bible--Meditations. | Christian life--Biblical teaching. | BISAC: RELIGION / Biblical Studies / Prophecy | RELIGION / Christian Living / Spiritual Growth
Classification: LCC BS491.5 .B44 2024 (print) | LCC BS491.5 (ebook) | DDC 242/.5--dc23/eng/20240329
LC record available at https://lccn.loc.gov/2024004115
LC ebook record available at https://lccn.loc.gov/2024004116

10 9 8 7 6 5 4 3 2 1

Published by Paraclete Press
Brewster, Massachusetts
www.paracletepress.com

Printed in the United States of America

CONTENTS

PART FOUR
WHEN HE *Opens* ...

FOREWORD

Jesus's disciples asked Him to teach them to pray. He responded by saying, *"Our Father, who art in heaven, hallowed be Thy name,"* then went on to explain how they needed to bring His will from heaven into the earth realm. Dr. Alemu's book, *When He Opens the Heavens: Responding to God's Invitation with Praise and Purpose*, is a wonderful tool to help you learn to pray.

Connecting heaven and earth releases the glory of God into our realm, and the release of that glory is no small thing! Moses cried out for it in Exodus 33:18, *"Show me Your glory!"* (NASB). The word for "glory" in Hebrew is *kabowd*, which means "weighty or heavy." Glory signifies authority. The word can also mean wealthy or prosperous, from the sense of being heavy with goods. When heaven and earth connect and God's glory is released, His weighty presence and great authority are tangible in this realm.

The New Testament word for glory, *doxa*, has in its root meaning the recognition of something—or someone—for what it really is. When the glory of the Lord is released, He is recognized! Saints and sinners alike will recognize Him, and His weighty presence will change things. A bold people will wear this glory. I think the greatest war ahead is in this realm. The enemy knows that if God's people are recognized as wearing His glory, the moving ark of His presence in them will dethrone Satan, just as the Ark of the Covenant toppled Dagon.

This is a time for us to "be" the people we read about in the book of Revelation. We need not be afraid to venture into new places where the Lord leads us. Many new doors of harvest will open in days ahead. We must be ready to go through, defy the enemy, release what he has captured, and restore it to God's rule and authority. Though many adversaries stand in our paths, our shield of faith will quench their fiery darts. Jeremiah 46:3 is encouraging: *"Prepare your shields, both large and small, and march out for battle!"* Let us go forth with confidence, with our shields lifted high, and our victory will be assured. It is time to break through, rise up, and advance into a new movement that rearranges history!

We are living in a time when we must open the gates for the King of Glory to come in. *"Lift up your heads, O you gates! And be lifted up, you everlasting doors! And the King of glory shall come in. Who is this King of glory? The LORD strong and mighty, the LORD mighty in battle. Lift up your heads, O you gates! Lift up, you everlasting doors! And the King of glory shall come in. Who is this King of glory? The LORD of hosts, He is the King of glory"* (Psalm 24:7–10).

The King of Glory is approaching the gate with His procession. Who is this King of Glory? He is the LORD of Hosts, Yahweh Sabaoth. The One with strength who can come through our gates and enable us to secure and defend our sphere of dominion. He is the Captain of all the angelic armies, the armies of Israel, the hosts of nations, ruler of everything in heaven and earth. When that heavenly portal opens, we allow this King access to our life, city, corporate worship, nation, and every sphere of our authority. Intercessors, take your stand! Open the portals of glory so He may come in. As you enter into the Throne Room with confidence and stand before the Father, you gain authority. As you stand on earth in the place the Lord has assigned you and connect with God's Presence in the Throne Room, you have authority to rebuild walls that have fallen.

Another word for gate is portal. A portal is a doorway, gate, or entrance, and there are many kinds. Even in our bodies, we have portal veins. These carry blood from our intestines and stomach to the liver, where it's filtered and then sent all through our body. The process is very intricate and complicated; however, the principle is the same. Once there is an opening, what comes through the opening can infiltrate all over. Therefore, if we open a door to God's Glory, we can stand in battle on His behalf and allow His fragrance to overcome the death all around us. Stand and open up the Portal of Glory and let the King of Glory in! Once the gates are opened, the "gatekeepers" of a city or territory can then fully execute God's plan. Open the gates! The King of Glory is ready to come in!

We are in a time of prophetic declaration and apostolic proclamation. God's people are becoming bold to say what He is saying. This creates an open heaven and brings heaven and earth into agreement. I call this an open portal or door in heaven. The book of Revelation provides deep insight into doors of heavenly access and the warfare that we will encounter. The apostle John had a supernatural visitation during an extreme time of persecution. In the midst of this persecution, he began to see that the Lord God omnipotent reigns! He recognized that those who would follow the Lord in their daily life would be involved in continuing spiritual conflict. As the Lord visited John, He gave him a message concerning the seven key churches of that region. This message also reveals to us God's heart concerning the Church today.

We then find John sharing with us in Revelation 4:1 the following: *"After these things, I looked, and behold, a door standing open in heaven. And the first voice which I heard was like a trumpet speaking with me, saying, 'Come up here, and I will show you things which must take place after this.'"* This open heaven causes our faith to soar. Faith overcomes! The shield of faith is closely related to the concept of a door—the Greek word is *thureos,* from *thura,* a square shield that can also be seen as a door. A door is an opening for entering or leaving a building, tent, or room. The door is used symbolically in the Bible in many ways. In Joshua 7:26, the Valley of Achor is a place of trouble, but later, in Hosea 2:15, it becomes "a door of hope," a reason for God's people to trust Him again. Our place of trouble can become the entry point into a new place of victory.

Jesus called Himself "the Door" (John 10:7, 9), and faith in Him is the only way to enter the kingdom of God. He calls all people to Himself, but He will not come in unless we open that door in faith (see Rev. 3:20). We need to give the Lord permission to take us through new, opportune doors, and He will give us the power to enter them successfully. Let us open the door of our hearts so that we can go through our new door of opportunity.

There are many doors of opportunity ahead for all of us and, as for the Apostle Paul, adversaries at each one—1 Corinthians 16:9, *"For a great and effective door has opened to me, and there are many adversaries."* Let us lift up our shield at the door! We do not need to be afraid to go through the opening and into the new places where the Lord will lead us. Even though many adversaries will be on our path in days ahead, our shield of faith will quench all of their fiery darts. *When He Opens the Heavens* will help you quench every fiery dart by keeping your shield of faith in place. This book will also help you make sure that important piece of armor is on you as you learn to pray the prayer of faith. Receive your ascension commission to live and walk from an open heaven!

—Dr. Chuck D. Pierce
President of Glory of Zion International, Kingdom Harvest Alliance

INTRODUCTION

The book you hold in your hands is born out of years of public ministry and a journey that has had many twists and turns, spanned numerous continents, and had an abundance of doors opened by the God of life. It is also born out of a deep reflection on biblical narratives on open heavens, open doors, open gates, and open hearts that embrace the spiritual power of a life in Christ.

During my years of ministry, many people have asked about my story. As I reflect on all that has happened in my life, I give glory to God for the great things He has done. But given my humble beginnings, even I question how so many incredible things have happened in my life. For example:

- How did I, having grown up in a remote farming community in Ethiopia, earn a PhD from one of the largest universities in the United States?
- How have I, raised in a pagan home, traveled to more than 54 nations teaching and preaching the gospel?
- How have I written more than 50 books?
- How could I possibly have envisioned the journey and future God had for me?

Those are just a few of the questions I'm asked when I teach and preach around the world. Typically, when I am asked, I give a brief response, yet people are amazed—and I am amazed as well! So many miracles have happened in my journey toward my prophetic destiny. I have written elsewhere (in the memoir *Breakout for Breakthrough*, 2019) in more detail about my story.

The call of God that I accepted 53 years ago still burns in my heart. That is why I am committed to continue preaching the gospel, training and equipping emerging leaders, encouraging and empowering the Body of Christ to fulfill the mandate of the gospel. And that is, above all else, why I have written *When He Opens the Heavens*.

In this book, I'm inviting you to much more than an understanding of how God has used me, a most unlikely vessel, for His good purposes. I'm inviting you to embrace your divine invitation from God and walk in obedience through the doors He opens, to fulfill your calling by opening the gates for the King of Glory, the Lord Jesus Christ. At the conclusion of each chapter, I have offered a few questions for reflection individually or in a small group context. For further clarification on the terms used in this book, at the end I have also provided a Note on Terms. I hope the words found in the pages that follow serve as a light for you on your path.

Amen! May it be so.

Alemu Beeftu

PART ONE

Open HEAVENS

CHAPTER 1

OPENING
AND CLOSING

The word "open" is a simple word we use daily in the English language. Yet, it's a powerful word in its implication, both spiritually and culturally. It is a rich word that has been used to express value, both metaphorically and practically, in daily life. Most things in life start with opening and closing, a beginning and an ending. Human life on earth begins when the birth canal opens to let out a baby. That is what we celebrate by calling it a birthday for the rest of our lives. Life ends with the closing of a coffin and the burial ground. Life starts with opening and finishes with closing. At birth we open our eyes and mouth; at death we shut our mouth and close our eyes. The dictionary[1] defines *open* and includes the following:

- having no enclosing or confining barrier; accessible on all or nearly all sides
- being in a position or adjustment to permit passage; not shut or locked
- completely free from concealment; exposed to general view or knowledge
- having no protective covering

---

1 Merriam-Webster's Collegiate Dictionary, Tenth Edition.

- not restricted to a particular group or category of participants
- fit to be traveled over; presenting no obstacle to passage or view
- having clarity and resonance unimpaired by undue tension or constriction of the throat
- available to follow or make use of
- characterized by ready accessibility and usually generous attitude; as generous in giving
- willing to hear and consider or to accept and deal, free from reserve or pretense
- being in operation (and so forth)

In the biblical context, the Hebrew word for open is הלָגָ, *gālāh*, "to uncover," referring to the opening of the eyes in vision (Numbers 22:31; 24:4). In the New Testament, the usual word is ἀνοίγω, *anoígō*, referring to the opening of mouth, eyes, heavens, doors, and so forth.[2]

Opening implies giving full access by removing all the obstacles or hindrances on all sides without restrictions. It is a sign of welcoming with an accepting attitude and a free-will invitation. Conversely, closing is preventing or denying entrance by restricting accessibility by shutting or blocking passageways.

The process of opening and closing is not limited to physical aspects of doors or gates. It also includes the unseen realm of authority. A person can open or close access or opportunities by using legal or spiritual authority. Jesus has been given all necessary authority to open and close since He was given the master key, called the key of David. "These are the words of him who is holy and true, who holds the key of David. What he opens no one can shut, and what he shuts no one can open" (Revelation 3:7). This is also true in the legal sense. Subsequently, everything starts with opening.

---

2 *International Standard Bible Encyclopedia.*

This is true for spiritual life and our relationship with the Lord. Jesus opened the heavens and came to give us access to the Father. He became the only entry point to having an eternal relationship with God. He referred to Himself as the only true door that no one can shut, for those who would like to come to the Father through Him. That is why He said, "I am the door; by me if any man enters in, he shall be saved, and shall go in and go out, and shall find pasture" (John 10:9, ASV).

We are born again when we open our heart to the Lord and invite Him in as our Lord and Savior without restriction. This opening of our heart also means a willingness to invite Him into our lives. It shows our availability to follow Him all the way with all our heart and live for His purpose and do His will on earth. We are a new creation because of the new relationship with Him. Our spiritual journey begins by coming to the Father through Jesus Christ, Who is the true door. The sign of our willingness to go through the open door, Jesus, is to open our lives and invite Him in to dwell with us by the person of the Holy Spirit. He knocks at the door of every person for a new beginning. When a person opens his heart to the Lord, the Lord opens the door of salvation for an eternal relationship. This individual is called to become a new creation.

Our spiritual well-being is the result of opening our lives to the Lord for ongoing fellowship. When we open our heart to Him, we give Him full access into our lives, since our heart is the entry point where Jesus came into our being. He comes to dwell in our heart by the person of the Holy Spirit. The Lord Jesus said, "Anyone who loves me will obey my teaching. My Father will love them, and we will come to them and make our home with them" (John 14:23). When we open our heart to Him, He comes to seal us for the day of salvation and dwell in us. That is what makes us a new creation. As a person opens their heart to the Lord, the Lord opens the heavens to a person to be seated on the throne with Him (Ephesians 2:6), and to enjoy all spiritual blessings in Jesus Christ in heavenly realms.

Salvation is the result of open heavens. The Lord Jesus came in the flesh to dwell among us to open the heavens, the dwelling place of God, as Jesus is the door of entrance. The desire and prayer of Prophet Isaiah was, "Oh, that you would rend the heavens and come down, that the mountains would tremble before you!" (Isaiah 64:1). Yes, the heavens were opened, and the curse was broken. The good news of salvation was declared by the angels on the day the Word became flesh in the tabernacle among us. Open heavens over us means a divine invitation to start a lasting relationship by opening our hearts to come and dwell in us and with us to establish His Kingly authority in our lives and on earth through us. That gives us not only authority but also responsibility to open the gates as a trusted servant for the King of Glory to come in and into our spheres of influence. This is called opening the gate for the King of Glory.

When we open our heart to the Lord, He opens the heavens over us by removing all the curses of sin and inequity for our blessing of having a lasting relationship with Him. That gives the authority and the key to open the gates for Him to come in. As the result of our ongoing relationship with Him as children, He gives us open doors to do His will on earth in obedience to His voice.

OPEN HEAVENS, DOORS AND GATES

Before we go too far in dealing with this topic, in the context of opening and closing, it is very important to look closely at the concepts of open heavens, open doors, and gates together, so we see the full picture. These three concepts have been mentioned throughout the Bible. Understanding their relationship and balancing among them is the key for our relationship to Him, as well as establishing our prophetic destiny and understanding our role in Kingdom work. Open heavens are a divine invitation for a relationship with Him for covenant and intimacy. Open doors are a divine invitation for our destiny to live a life of obedience, to run the race faithfully, to be fruitful for the glory of God. Open gates are a divine invitation for the Kingdom mandate to honor Him as we prepare the way for the full manifestation for the nations to see and honor the King of Glory, Who is coming soon.

When He opens the heavens over us for a true and lasting relationship that is being established, fellowship is affirmed. A true identity is being realized for God's blessings to be released and for His approval to be declared. When He opens doors, the calling is realized and a true commission for the purpose of God is affirmed to do His will and fulfill His purpose on earth. The bridge between the heavens and earth becomes tangible, and the Lord's prayer is answered. "Let your will be done on earth as it is in heaven." This gives kingdom workers the keys of the kingdom to open the gate for the King of Glory to come in, as well as their receiving the authority to speak to the ancient gates to open up. "Lift up your heads, you gates; be lifted up, you ancient doors, that the King of glory may come in" (Psalm 24:7). He comes in to reign and rule. This is the proclamation of Revelation 11:15, spoken with loud voices in Heaven.

> "The kingdom of the world has become the kingdom of our Lord and of his Messiah, and he will reign for ever and ever."

Open heavens over you are a divine invitation (Revelation 4:1), not only for a new relationship but also for a lasting relationship, while open doors represent the opportunities He provides to be fruitful for us to walk through in obedience and by faith to fulfill our calling. The core of our calling and prophetic destiny to declare the glory of King Jesus on earth is opening the gates and introducing Him as the King of kings and Lord of lords and the Savior of the world.

CONCEPTUAL FRAMEWORK

As we look closely at these interrelated concepts of opening, let us make a firm decision. First, stay under open heavens by protecting our ongoing relations and responding to the heavenly invitation, "Come up here" (Revelation 4:1). Second, receive the power of the Holy Spirit and the revelation of His Word to know and walk through open doors that He places before us every day in spirit obedience and sincere faith (Revelation 3:7–8). Third, know our values with a biblically based belief system, establish our identity, and commit to our purpose. They make us in the Kingdom of God a VIP (an individual with value, identity, and purpose), creating a difference in our generation by service, fulfilling His purpose and impacting our generation for the glory of God.

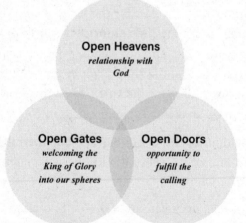

Open Heavens
relationship with God

Open Gates
welcoming the King of Glory into our spheres

Open Doors
opportunity to fulfill the calling

With that conceptual framework in our hearts and minds, let's go deeper into the open heavens and our desire for God's presence in our world.

Questions for Reflection and Discussion

1. What does it mean to "open our hearts" to God?
2. In what ways have you seen your own spiritual well-being connected directly to fellowship with the Lord?
3. In what ways have you perceived yourself as being a "kingdom worker"? How does that motivate you in your spiritual life?

CHAPTER 2

OPEN HEAVENS

The concept of open heavens is a desire for God's presence among His people to protect, guide, provide, and create genuine, tangible signs of His presence through His acts of mercy and grace. Closed heavens are about God's judgment, while open heavens signify His mercy and compassion.

The first family, Adam and Eve, started under an open heaven with God. But because of sin, they were put out not only from the Garden of Eden but also from fellowship with God. The closing of the garden was also a picture of the closing of the heavens. That resulted in curses, rather than blessings. "Cursed is the ground because of you; through painful toil you will eat food from it all the days of your life" (Genesis 3:17). Since that time, every sincere follower of God desires to have the same kind of fellowship with God, under open heavens. This same desire was also the prayer of the prophets, "Oh, that you would rend the heavens and come down, that the mountains would tremble before you!" (Isaiah 64:1). Ezekiel started his ministry under this type of an open heaven. "The heavens were opened and I saw visions of God" (Ezekiel 1:1). As a result, he started under open heavens where he experienced the special touch of God. "There the hand of the LORD was upon him" (Ezekiel 1:3). Other open heaven passages are cited throughout the Bible.

Open heavens are about the manifested presence of God in the context of our relationship with Him. They are about knowing Him and establishing our personal identity and affirming our prophetic destiny to fulfill our divine purpose on earth because of our relationship with the God of an everlasting covenant. The concept of open heavens can't be a reality without understanding and walking in a covenant relationship, since it's a restoration of divine presence and the Lord's goodness. In a covenant, God opens the heavens over us while He opens doors before us, so that as His children, we can open the gates of our lives, ministries, cities, and nations for the establishment of His Kingdom authority! (Psalm 24:7–10). Yes, open heavens affirm covenantal relationship for a greater, deeper revelation that leads to true restoration for lasting transformation in every dimension of our lives.

ABRAHAM AND OPEN HEAVENS

The concept of an open heaven became a reality when God revealed Himself to Abram and called him to leave his country of birth, his people, and his father's household and follow God to go to the place He would show him. This calling started with a promise: "Go to the land I will show you." In other words, Abraham's calling started with a vision of the future hope and inheritance, which is a true sign of an open heaven. In this context, open heavens include the voice of God: "The LORD said to Abram"; the leading of God: "I will show you"; and promises of God, His covenant: "I will . . .," two words the Lord repeated seven times in declaring what He would do for Abram. What a covenant relationship! From this point on, Abram walked with the revelation of God, with an unbreakable covenant, under open heavens. That is the reason we read phrases like these:

"The LORD appeared to Abram" (Genesis 12:7)
"So he built an altar there to the LORD, who had appeared
to him" (Genesis 12:7)
"The LORD said to Abram . . ., 'Look around from where
you are . . .'" (Genesis 13:14)

When the Lord came to Abram in a vision, He also showed
him not only the Promised Land for the coming generation but
also his descendants under an open heaven, showing him the
stars and promising him his descendants would be like the stars.

With this unique relationship with God, under an open
heaven, Abram's identity was established and sealed forever
through the circumcision he received as a sign of a lasting
covenant. This permanent change of his identity was reflected
in the change of his name. "As for me, this is my covenant with
you: You will be the father of many nations. No longer will you
be called Abram; your name will be Abraham, for I have made
you a father of many nations" (Genesis 17:4–5). The physical
circumcision he received when he was 99 years old became the
covenant sign between him and God.

This unique relationship with God, under open heavens,
gave Abram the opportunity to become a friend of God with
his new identity. "But you, Israel, my servant, Jacob, whom I
have chosen, you descendants of Abraham my friend" (Isaiah
41:8; see also 2 Chronicles 20:7).

Abraham, under open heavens, had a significant relationship
with the Creator of the heavens and the earth. Consequently, he
had an everlasting covenant that gave him not only promises
of future blessings but also a new identity that made him a
blessing to the nations. He became the worshiper and friend
of God. Open heavens are an invitation to know God and have
a new vision about God's plans and purposes and accept our
true identity to fulfill our calling and become the channel of His

blessings to our generation. Open heavens are the starting point for both true identity and fruitfulness.

JACOB AND OPEN HEAVENS

Jacob is the first person in the Old Testament who had an open heaven vision in a dream. Open heavens, among other things, are a place of the clear vision of God, and a place for the clear voice of God. Jacob was Abraham's grandson. The Lord chose Jacob to fulfill what he promised His friend Abraham. The God of Jacob, among other things, is the God of prophetic destiny. In my opinion, among all the Bible characters, no one fought for his prophetic destiny like Jacob. However, Jacob was mostly misunderstood—by his own family at birth and by others in the coming years.

Jacob received His prophetic destiny before he was born because of what God had promised Abraham. "The LORD said to her: 'Two nations are in your womb; two people will come from you and be separated. One people will be stronger than the other, and the older will serve the younger'" (Genesis 25:23, HCSB).

Isaac prayed for a child, and his wife, Rebekah, became pregnant. It was an unusual pregnancy, because while in Rebekah's womb, the two boys started wrestling for their prophetic destiny. When she asked the Lord what was going on, the Lord told her that there were two nations in her womb, and "The older will serve the younger." In other words, the younger will be a leader. That prophecy entered into Jacob's spirit, and from that time on Jacob started fighting for his prophetic destiny. He was born with a prophetic destiny, even though he didn't understand it, as is the case for every person. That prophetic destiny became the driving force in Jacob's life, making him a wrestler or a fighter, as well as a restless man.

OPEN HEAVENS FOR PROPHETIC DESTINY

A person can't have true rest until the realization of what God has created each one to accomplish is brought to light. Open heavens bring to light our prophetic destiny. God reveals that prophetic destiny to individuals in different ways and at different stages of life, but everyone is born with a prophetic destiny, just like Jacob. The Bible says, "Seeking the God of Jacob," rather than the God of Abraham or Isaac. We know that the name "God of Abraham" refers to the God of covenant. Abraham is the one who received the covenant and walked with God. He is also called the "God of Isaac," which means the God of promises or blessings. Abraham received the covenant, and Isaac received the blessings of the covenant. Jacob, on the other hand, received his prophetic destiny and later entered into the full revelation for future blessings. What God promised both Abraham and Isaac was fully realized in the life of Jacob under open heavens. The nation of covenant is called by Jacob's prophetic destiny name, Israel, a picture of a new identity and an everlasting covenant relationship.

The prophetic word—the promises or call of God—is your weapon to fight against everything that tries to stop you from reaching your destiny. This is usually referred to as hearing the call of God. When we receive a revelation of God's plan for our lives and embrace that plan, we are on our way. In some cases, the Lord places that prophetic destiny in a person, and it becomes like a burning fire. To some, God gives a burden or care for things related to their prophetic destiny, and this makes them restless. God uses that to guide an individual to their prophetic destiny, just like Jacob.

Jacob received his prophetic destiny before he was born. Even though he was too young to understand what the Lord declared over him about being a leader, God's prophetic word became a fire in his bones by creating a passion in him to see the fulfillment of his prophetic destiny. His prophetic destiny and passion were from the Lord, but the method he engaged in to see their fulfillment was wrong until he had a true encounter with the God of Abraham and Isaac under an open heaven. Before Jacob moved on, the Lord had to deal with his carnal efforts under open heavens. Before the divine encounter, under his open heavens experience, he tried the following methods to fulfill his prophetic destiny:

- **Using his own strength to fight for his prophetic destiny**
  In the womb, Jacob started wrestling with his twin brother, Esau, for position. Jacob wanted to be the firstborn to gain the role of a leader, and he fought until the last minutes of their birth. When his brother went ahead of him in their mother's birth canal, Jacob tried to pull Esau back in a final attempt to be the firstborn. Jacob's enemy was not Esau. In fact, according to Jacob's prophetic destiny, Esau was born to serve Jacob. Take note: Using the wrong method can hinder what was created to serve you so that you can reach your prophetic destiny.

- **Using resources to buy his prophetic destiny**
  Jacob thought that his prophetic destiny of being a leader was related directly to being firstborn. It wasn't. God did not promise Jacob to be the firstborn, but to be a leader. However, the cultural tradition of being the firstborn for a double inheritance influenced Jacob's worldview. Since he wasn't successful in holding back his brother to be the firstborn, Jacob's strategy was to buy the birthright from his brother in order to fulfill his prophetic destiny. In this setting, the brothers are a picture of generations that try to fulfill their purpose without experiencing open heavens, knowing God, and establishing their identity. The first tries to achieve prophetic destiny through creative strategies. The second misuses the gift of God for temporary gain. When

we try to sell or buy the precious gift of God, we make it valueless. Destiny can't be bought, and the gift of God can't be sold. Focus often switches from God's glory and Kingdom work to human glory and personal gain when individuals or organizations reach this stage. That is one of the reasons why the Lord searches for someone who will prioritize His glory and reestablish His eternal purpose by restoring the love of God more than anything else by being under open heavens.

- **Using skills to deceive his father**
  What Jacob tried to do at this point didn't change anything in his life. The path to prophetic destiny is not what a person wrestles with in an attempt to gain inner peace or what they get through deception, but rather involves internal transformation. When Isaac told Esau to hunt and prepare wild game and bring it to him so that he could eat and bless him, Isaac was asking Esau for a point of contact so Esau could receive the blessings that would come from honoring Isaac. When Rebekah heard what Isaac told Esau, she didn't waste any time before telling Jacob the principle of giving and receiving. She instructed Jacob on how to receive Isaac's blessings. All Jacob's life, his inner cry was to receive the firstborn's blessing to reach his prophetic destiny. Nothing was wrong in Jacob when he went to his father to receive the blessing; the problem was the method he and his mother devised. Their core strategy was to deceive Isaac so that Jacob could receive the blessings that were intended for Esau. This is another sign of starting in the wrong place. The problems are twofold. First, when we try to use shortcuts to reach our prophetic destiny, we lack integrity of character. Second, when we try to get what we think we need to fulfill our call without honesty and transparency, we open doors for spirits of deception and corruption. We could end up like Jacob, even after we receive what we seek, running away in fear from our inheritance.

Jacob received what he searched for all his life under open heavens. God affirmed his covenant to Jacob under open heavens. Under open heavens, he not only received a vision of heaven, but he also received the awareness of the presence of God. The answer came under open heavens!

As we continue together, let's look at a starting place under open heavens—a place called Bethel.

Questions for Reflection and Discussion

1. How do the stories of Abraham and Jacob speak to you about the concept of "open heavens"? What is surprising to you? What is challenging?
2. How have you experienced "the prophetic word" (the promises or call of God) in your life?
3. How have you responded?

CHAPTER 3

BETHEL AS A PLACE OF OPEN HEAVENS

He had a dream in which he saw a stairway resting on the earth, with its top reaching to heaven, and the angels of God were ascending and descending on it. . . . "I am with you and will watch over you wherever you go, and I will bring you back to this land. I will not leave you until I have done what I have promised you." . . . **He called that place Bethel.**

—Genesis 28:12, 15, 19, emphasis added

BETHEL—A STARTING PLACE UNDER OPEN HEAVEN

Jacob, a man of prophetic destiny, spent many years in the village of his birth, where he tried his best to make his prophetic destiny happen on his own. His parents' home and village, where he grew up, were not places of the full revelation of his prophetic destiny. They were, however, the place where he started the search for his true prophetic identity. One day, he was forced to leave that familiar place and environment because of the threat of his brother, Esau.

Gilgal is a place of total freedom for a journey of prophetic destiny, while Bethel is a place of revelation for what is ahead. For a prophetic journey, Bethel is a picture of a place of the following:

1. **Covenant, Genesis 28:10-22**

   After so many years of struggling to make his prophetic destiny happen, Jacob reached Bethel and lay down to spend the night. The place was not comfortable; in fact, his pillow was a stone. But it was the most important place for his prophetic destiny. What made this particular place so important was that Abraham, Jacob's grandfather, had done the same years before. Abraham had built an altar of worship to God, Who had revealed Himself to Abraham and had given a promise: "To your offspring I will give this land" (Genesis 12:7). God kept that promise. When Jacob spent the night in Bethel, God revealed Himself to Jacob in a dream.

   The altar of worship we build today is a place of revelation for the next generation of tomorrow. Furthermore, the place of the true altar of worship gives the next generation victory to take back what the enemy stole in past generations. We see this in Joshua 8:12-29. Joshua conquered the enemy that had defeated his people previously in Bethel.

2. **Revelation about the God of covenant, Genesis 28:12**

   That night Jacob had a dream for the first time. It was a prophetic dream about his future, as well as his relationship with the God of Abraham and Isaac. The dream depicted an open heaven with a connecting ladder to earth. The ladder of Jacob's destiny came down to him without any struggle on his part. Jacob saw the angels of the Lord ascending and descending on the ladder. That ladder was the Lord Jesus Christ in the Old Testament. Jesus Himself said, "Very truly I tell you, you will see 'heaven open, and the angels of God ascending and descending on' the Son of Man" (John 1:51). Prophetic destiny can only be fulfilled through Christ Jesus, Who gives us access to the presence of God through His death and resurrection. He is the only way and the only door to our prophetic destiny.

3. Divine appointment

Jacob received his prophetic destiny before he was born, but he had never heard the Lord's voice through all his struggles until he reached Bethel. That night in his prophetic dream he heard, "I am the LORD, the God of your father Abraham and the God of Isaac" (Genesis 28:13).

This was the most important statement for Jacob for a number of reasons. First, it established his connection to God's covenant promises. Jacob knew without a shadow of doubt that he was in the plan and purpose of God. Second, it established the authority of God: "I am the LORD." The Lord was saying to Jacob that He is the One Who called Abraham and entered into an everlasting covenant with him. Jacob is part of this covenant! This divine appointment was to establish this covenant with Jacob. Third, it showed that the Lord was in control of Jacob's destiny. There above it stood the Lord, who proclaimed, "I will give you and your descendants the land on which you are lying" (Genesis 28:13). In spite of the struggle Jacob went through, the Lord was telling him, "Your prophetic destiny is secured."

Every prophetic destiny the Lord gives us comes with full assurance of fulfillment because of the faithfulness of the Promise Giver. The Apostle Paul affirmed this eternal truth, "The one who calls you is faithful, and he will do it" (1 Thessalonians 5:24). Paul also reminded us, "No matter how many promises God has made, they are 'Yes' in Christ" (2 Corinthians 1:20). When we receive this truth, we start living life in obedience instead of trying to fight the wrong war. Remember, our war is not with flesh and blood. We win the spiritual war by the authority of the Name of the Lord and because of our relationship with Him. Our spiritual authority is a result of our anointing, while anointing is a fruit of an ongoing relationship. An increase in glory is not available without total obedience to the revealed will of God.

4. Confirmation of prophetic destiny

The Lord went beyond Jacob, telling Jacob about his descendants possessing the land. This is about future vision. That is why it is called prophetic destiny. There is no prophetic destiny without true vision. That is the reason people perish where there is no vision. Without vision there is no future hope.

Hopelessness is the most harmful disease in human life. Hopelessness leads to powerlessness, which makes a person vulnerable. After a while that becomes a difficult cycle to break. That is what we witnessed when we read about the journey of the Israelites in the wilderness. They traveled around the same mountain for about 38 years until the Lord came and told them to break camp and move forward (Deuteronomy 1). They had lost vision for their prophetic destiny.

One of the most important things about Bethel is receiving or confirming prophetic destiny. Part of confirming our prophetic destiny is the release of future covenant blessings. Such covenant blessings include these (Genesis 28:14–15):

• Multiplication of descendants
• Divine guidance
• Protection
• Fulfillment of the promises
• Provision

Jacob woke up with this declaration over him in Bethel. All these blessings were pronounced over him in one night.

5. **God's presence**

The most powerful part of the Bethel revelation, relating to our prophetic journey, is experiencing God's presence at the highest level. "When Jacob awoke from his sleep, he thought, 'Surely the LORD is in this place, and I was not aware of it.' He was afraid and said, 'How awesome is this place! This is none other than the house of God; this is the gate of heaven'" (Genesis 28:16–17). The journey of prophetic destiny is not about what we will do at our destination, but what we will become in the process because of encountering God on the journey. As a result of his encounter with God, the great experience of the holy fear of God entered Jacob. He left his father's house because of the fear of his brother. At Bethel he experienced the true fear of God. The fear of God is the beginning of wisdom to discern our prophetic destiny. That desert place became the gate of heaven for Jacob to enter into the presence of God. He was more overwhelmed by the presence of God than by what was spoken about his future. He said, "How awesome is this place!" That is what the Bethel journey is all about.

6. **Worship**

The awesome presence of God led Jacob into true worship. He had never built an altar of worship before. But after that experience, he took his pillow, made an altar, and poured oil on it. He called that place the house of God, also known as Bethel. The house of God is a place of worship for the nations. By doing this, Jacob accepted his prophetic destiny and embraced his future. He promised the Lord he would make that place the house of God and would honor God with his tithing (Genesis 28:18–22). The Bethel revelation enables us to set our priorities straight and to learn how to honor God.

God is no respecter of persons. This means that what He did for Jacob, He will do for each of us. Jacob had no warning or awareness that God was going to visit him on that particular night in the desert. However, when he had the dream, he was receptive and alert to what God was showing him. Our revelation of Bethel may be a surprise as well, but if we remain watchful and obedient to His Spirit, we won't miss our opportunity to have an awesome experience with Him. In the meantime, pray and seek the Lord continually. Establish your own altar of worship and stay in His presence. When you hear the Lord's voice or sense His presence, enter in and listen to His voice. Record what you hear him saying, so you can pray and seek greater revelation to pursue your vision. These are exciting times in which we live.

BETHEL:
A FINISHING PLACE UNDER OPEN HEAVENS

It was time for Jacob to go back to Bethel and move beyond the deceptive and costly comfort in the land of the Hivites. Because of the prophetic destiny on Jacob's life, the Lord intervened. God said to Jacob, "Go up to Bethel and settle there, and build an altar there to God, who appeared to you when you were fleeing from your brother Esau" (Genesis 35:1). In my opinion, this is the most important verse for a person who would like to start and finish under open heavens. This is about completing a cycle of prophetic journey in order to dwell in a place of relationship, revelation, and true identity for covenantal blessings. When Jacob was in the wrong place, not only did he fail to build an altar to the Lord, but he also failed to protect his home from the idols coming in.

We can't fulfill our prophetic destiny without building and renewing the true altar of worship. The core of our prophetic destiny is a living relationship with our Father, the King of Glory. A living relationship requires a pure altar and the fresh fire of the Holy Spirit. Revelation is a result of the Holy Spirit's presence in our lives. The Lord in His eternal mercy came back to rescue Jacob and told him three things:

1. **Go Up!**

   This was a command, not a suggestion. God is serious about His plan and purpose in our lives. He expects us to complete the journey in His right time and to dwell in the right place. Get up! Wake up! Arise and go! These are commands that show a change of time and season. A new season is clearly a time of transition from the old to the new.

   Transition is a time of change. It is for right alignment with God's purpose and call. Being in the right place at the right time is part of the transition process.

2. **Go to Bethel**

   For Jacob, Bethel was a place of revelation where the Lord revealed Himself to him as the God of Abraham and Isaac. It was a place of revelation about God Himself, the next generation, and the land itself. It was where Jacob heard God's voice for the first time. It was a place of his true dream, where heaven and earth came together with the ladder from heaven, a prophetic picture of Jesus Christ. Bethel was a place of divine appointment for Jacob to overcome his human effort and surrender to God's will. It was a place of personal encounter with the Creator of the heavens and the earth. It was a place of entering into the court of heaven to hear the decision of the King of Glory. "This is none other than the house of God; this is the gate of heaven" (Genesis 28:17). It is a picture of the throne room of the King of kings. It is a place for renewal of focus and purpose, and a place that confirms prophetic destiny. Bethel is the house of God, where His presence is real and His majesty is overwhelming. This place shows the light of His glory and the purity of His holiness. It is a place of holy reverence where God is honored, and a place for the true altar of worship. These are some of the reasons the Lord commanded Jacob to get up and go back to Bethel.

Bethel is not only a place of receiving the revelation of our prophetic destiny, but it's also a place to dwell for the rest of our lives. If we don't dwell in Bethel, we start living on past experience at the expense of today's revelation. That is the problem with religion. When we don't live in a relationship and with revelation, we build monuments for past encounters instead of creating the movement necessary to fulfill our prophetic destiny. That is the difference between the spirit of religion and a living relationship with the God of revelation.

3. **Build an Altar**
   Jacob could have built an altar for God among the Hivites, but it was necessary for him to return to Bethel. The altar is a result of the revelation of Who God is. Abraham built an altar to the Lord, Who revealed Himself to him. Worship without the revelation of Who God is results in simply going through ritual without the manifestation of God's reality. The foundation of a true altar of worship is revelation of the Holy Spirit and the cleansing blood of Jesus Christ.

In obedience to the voice of God, Jacob told his family to get ready to go back to Bethel. First, they would purge themselves of the foreign gods they worshiped. They collected those and brought them to Jacob. As a sign of true repentance, he buried the foreign gods. Burial of past sin is a true sign of transitioning into the new. Second, they purified themselves. By barring idols, they cleansed themselves from the past. Through the act of purification, they consecrated or set themselves apart to the Lord. One is not complete without the other. Yes, we need to get rid of past sin, and at the same time we need to rededicate ourselves to Him and start living with Him and for Him. This is a process of renewing our minds so that His Spirit will guide our souls into the fullness of Christ.

Then they set out on the journey to Bethel. There, Jacob would build the altar to God and his family would settle in a place of revelation. As they started the journey, God's presence came to lead them. With the presence of God, "The terror of God fell upon the towns all around them so that no one pursued them" (Genesis 35:5). God's presence became their shield. On arriving at Bethel, "He built an altar, and he called the place El Bethel, because it was there that God revealed Himself to him when he was fleeing from his brother" (Genesis 35:7).

"El Bethel" means "the God of Bethel." The significance of this name is that it is not about revelation or a prophetic dream anymore, but about the God of revelation. It is very easy to worship the event instead of the Lord of all miracles.

After Jacob built the altar, the Lord appeared to him again. The first time the Lord appeared to Jacob it was to give him the dream of revelation to establish his prophetic destiny. That was a confirmation of his call and purpose in his life.

The second time the Lord established Jacob's identity by giving him a new name. This was about the transformation of his life for character qualification for his prophetic destiny. With the call and anointing of God, we need character to accomplish His will on earth and bring glory to His name.

The third appearance was for blessing. "God appeared to him again and blessed him" (Genesis 35:9). When we are in our prophetic destiny, we are ready for the "again time." This again time is the release of the full blessings of God—including personal victory, fruitfulness, increase and multiplication, generational blessings, inheritances, and future hope. These blessings were given to Jacob when he came back to the right place. Adam and Eve received similar blessings in the Garden (Genesis 1). Noah also received such a blessing after he came out of the ark (Genesis 9).

The great blessing of such appearances is the manifested presence of God; that is, the blessings of being found in the field. Ruth is a great picture of this. When Boaz found her in his field, she received 22 different blessings, as I wrote in my book *Determination to Make a Difference*. We witness in the book of Mark similar things when the disciples went out to declare the good news of Christ's resurrection. "The disciples went out and preached everywhere, and the Lord worked with them and confirmed his word by the signs that accompanied it" (Mark 16:20).

This is the again time for the Body of Christ. Starting in Bethel, under open heavens, is not enough, unless we are willing to pay the price to finish in Bethel. The again time is to go back to the place of open heavens for revelation and divine visitation for our second chance. That is one of the reasons why the concept of an open heaven is so important for this hour.

And so the question I pose to you is this: Are you prepared to go back to your Bethel?

Questions for Reflection and Discussion

1. How have you experienced God's presence "at the highest level" as Jacob did in Bethel?

2. God is no respecter of persons. That means what He did for Jacob, He will do for each of us. How do you respond to this? Is this promise new to you? Is it reassuring?

3. What would it mean to consecrate yourself to the Lord?

CHAPTER 4

MOUNT SINAI AS A PLACE OF OPEN HEAVENS

What the Lord started with Abraham, established through Isaac, and demonstrated through Jacob's life journey—the covenant—became the standard for the Israelites. The Lord's desire for the nation of Israel, through their history, was to stay under the open heaven to experience the blessings in order to be the channel of His blessings and light to the nations of the world.

JOURNEY UNDER OPEN HEAVENS

The Lord brought the Israelites out of Egypt to have an ongoing relationship through true worship. The message to Pharaoh made God's plan for His people so clear from the beginning when He said, "Let my people go, so that they may worship me in the wilderness" (Exodus 7:16). True worship takes place only under open heavens. The Lord brought them out of slavery with a mighty hand to receive their worship and to reveal Himself as the God of Abraham, the God of Isaac, and the God of Jacob, and as their father. "Then say to Pharaoh, 'This is what the LORD says: Israel is my firstborn son, and I told you, "Let my son go, so he may worship me"""" (Exodus 4:22–23). The Lord used comparable words when He testified about the Lord Jesus under open heavens: "This is my Son, whom I love; with him I am well pleased" (Matthew 3:17). As I mentioned before, open heavens are about connection and relationship. The Lord delivered the Israelites in order to have ongoing covenantal relationships under open heavens. They were led on their journey of freedom by a pillar of fire and cloud to show He was with them and for them.

OPEN HEAVENS AT MOUNT SINAI

After they were on the journey of freedom under open heavens for three months, the Lord showed them His greater glory under open heavens by fulfilling what He promised Moses during the interaction at the burning bush. "I will be with you. And this will be the sign to you that it is I who have sent you: When you have brought the people out of Egypt, you will worship God on this mountain" (Exodus 3:12). When they arrived at Mount Sinai, the Lord opened the heavens in a very special way to receive their worship and fellowship. For the people of covenant, open heavens are a place of worshiping God in Spirit and in Truth.

Another sign of open heavens is the voice of God. The Lord called Moses to the top of the mountain and told him to remind the people about how he delivered them from slavery. God carried them on eagles' wings to Himself at Mount Sinai. God promised to make them His treasured possession, a Kingdom of priests and a holy nation, if they obeyed Him and kept His covenant. The people were to worship Him and be set apart for Him. Worshiping the Lord under open heavens releases upon us His blessings and healing power. Moses told the Israelites, "Worship the LORD your God, and his blessing will be on your food and water. I will take away sickness from among you" (Exodus 23:25). After they crossed over the Red Sea, the Lord promised He would not bring any diseases that He had brought on their enemies. He promised to be their healer, as long as they stayed under open heavens in obedience to His laws and protected their relationship with Him through sincere worship.

The visitation of God on Mount Sinai gave true revelation of Who He is and the plan and purpose He had for them. Before they arrived at Mount Sinai, Moses told them to prepare for the third day when the Lord would come down with thunder and lightning, along with a thick cloud and a very loud trumpet as a sign of open heavens. When God's presence came, His covenant came. "Mount Sinai was covered with smoke, because the LORD descended on it in fire. The smoke billowed up from it like smoke from a furnace, and the whole mountain trembled violently" (Exodus 19:18). After the amazing, awesome presence of God, Moses brought the people out of their camp to meet with God under the open heavens. The Lord spoke from the fire, and they heard His voice without being consumed by the fire and holiness of God. "The LORD our God has shown us his glory and his majesty, and we have heard his voice from the fire" (Deuteronomy 5:24). One of the greatest signs of open heavens is the manifestation of His glorious presence in a tangible way. What an unbelievable day of open heavens for people who had been in slavery under closed heavens for 400 years.

After this open-heavens experience, the Lord called Moses to the top of the mountain, and Moses went to the top of Mount Sinai, where God's glorious presence manifested. "Moses was there with the Lord forty days and forty nights without eating bread or drinking water" (Exodus 34:28). During his time with the Lord on top of Mount Sinai under open heavens, some powerful things took place.

First, Moses was transformed. When he came down from the mountain after being with God for forty nights and days, his face was shining with the glory of God. The Israelites could not look steadily at his face because of its glory. He had to put a veil over his face in order to approach the people.

Second, Moses talked with God face to face. God Himself testified to this truth. "With him I speak face to face" (Numbers 12:8). In another place, this account is also given: "The LORD would speak to Moses face to face, as one speaks with his friend. Then Moses would return to the camp" (Exodus 33:11). What a testimony for a leader who was appointed and sent to deliver the people of covenant and bring them to a place where they too were able to hear God's voice.

Third, Moses received not only the revelation of God's word but also the written word of God. God wrote on tablets the words of His covenant, the Ten Commandments, and gave them to Moses to deliver to the people. True understanding of God's eternal word and an impactful message came under open heavens. That is why staying under open heavens is not optional for those who are committed to God's purposes and would like to make a difference in their generation.

Fourth, he received the pattern to build the tabernacle on the mountain under the open heavens.

> "Have them make a sanctuary for me, and I will dwell among them. Make this tabernacle and all its furnishings exactly like the pattern I will show you."
> —Exodus 25:8–9

Through this, the Lord extended the open-heavens experience by making a decision to dwell among His people. The highest, deepest experience of open heavens is the dwelling presence of God. The Lord asked the people to make a sanctuary while they were still on their journey in the wilderness. Of course, for God to come and dwell among them, He needed a place as a point of connection. That preparation was to welcome the manifestation of God's presence: their Father, the God of Abraham, the God of Isaac, and the God of Jacob.

In the Bible, the Lord gave Moses the second detailed pattern that He gave to a man for building. The first pattern was given to Noah to build the ark to save his family. The second was for Moses to build the tabernacle—or sanctuary or tent of meeting with God. The experience of salvation without God's presence is not complete. The beauty and power of salvation is to return God's presence and His reality.

The designer of the pattern for the tabernacle was God, not man. The original plan was created by God to fully express His eternal plan and desire to continue the friendship He had started with Abraham. That was the reason He showed His special pattern to Moses to build the tabernacle for Him to dwell among God's covenant people. After Abraham, who was the friend of God, Moses became very close to God and saw His glory. In other words, Moses became a friend of God just like Abraham, through faith and his daily walk with Him. Furthermore, God found Moses to be a faithful servant for the house of God. "Just as Moses was faithful in all God's house . . . Moses was faithful as a servant in all God's house" (Hebrews 3:2, 5). True faith and a close walk with God produced godly character.

When God found Moses to be a close friend and faithful servant who obeyed according to what was shown to him, God revealed a detailed pattern for the tabernacle to Moses. Building a tabernacle was God's plan to fulfill His desire to dwell among His people because of His covenant and love. This is a very important point to underline and to understand. The concept of open heavens is of foremost importance. God longs to be with and among His people even more than we desire to be in His presence.

Additionally, God is looking for a friend to release a pattern—someone who invites or releases the manifestation of His presence. To receive the pattern, Moses became a close friend of God, who was faithful in the house of God. Friendship was about Moses's relationship with God, while His faithfulness was about Moses's character. These are key in receiving a pattern that brings the presence of God.

Furthermore, Moses received the pattern on the mountain. "See that you make them according to the pattern shown you on the mountain" (Exodus 25:40). Moses went to the mountain to receive a message from the Lord for God's people. Moses approached God to hear the Word of God and to be in God's presence for a long period of time. Sometimes, he stayed on the mountain in the presence of God for forty days and nights without eating or drinking, as I have mentioned before.

"Moses entered the cloud as he went on up the mountain. And he stayed on the mountain forty days and forty nights" (Exodus 24:18). On the mountain the Lord gave Moses the pattern to build the tabernacle for Him. In other words, Moses experienced the presence of God before He received the pattern for the tabernacle. Relationship should precede an assignment or even a commission or mandate that God has given us.

Open heavens are not just for personal edification, but to receive the pattern to build what can host the glorious presence of God. The call of God is to "come up here." On the mountain of God, we don't see anything else except the glory of God. We only hear the voice of God. His presence transforms us into the image of God, just as it did with Moses.

Once a person has an open-heaven experience on the mountain in His presence, they will be transformed into His image to reflect His glory and live for the praises of His name. That is the main reason to be under open heavens. Many leaders get their pattern from their personal experiences, education, training, or culture. Very few people are willing to pay the price to go up on the mountain of God to be transformed in His presence and receive a pattern to build what will host His presence.

There is a purpose to the building of the tabernacle and its connection to open heavens. It is to that topic we now turn our focus.

Questions for Reflection and Discussion

1. What about the story of Moses, as portrayed in this chapter, stood out the most to you? Why?

2. "Worshiping the Lord under open heavens releases upon us His blessings and healing power." How have you seen this truth in your own life or in the lives of others?

3. What might be the cost of "going up on the mountain of God to be transformed in His presence" in this day, in your context?

CHAPTER 5

THE TABERNACLE AS A PLACE OF OPEN HEAVENS

The Lord told Moses, clearly, that the purpose of the tabernacle would be just as He told Noah the purpose of the ark was to be: the tabernacle was for the Lord to dwell among His people, and He declared, "I will dwell among them." He showed them His manifested presence so they would be able to worship Him. The tabernacle established a path to approach a Holy God and worship Him with all their mind, soul, and strength.

UNDERSTANDING THE PURPOSE OF THE TABERNACLE

Through the tabernacle, the Lord showed the priority and standard of worship. The worship of God can't be placed on the back burner. It can't wait until we arrive at our destiny or destination. We can't hold back the worship of God. The Lord didn't wait until God's people came to the Promised Land to establish a system of worship. He showed them how to worship Him according to His standard during their journey in the wilderness. Even those who didn't enter the Promised

Land worshiped Him as they wandered in the wilderness. God delivered them so that they would be able to worship Him. In order to worship Him in spirit and in truth, they needed to know how to approach this awesome, holy God.

God, by nature, is a devouring fire. He dwells in unapproachable light and glory. Through the tabernacle, He showed them how to come into His presence and offer sacrifices of praise without being consumed by His holiness. He taught them how to seek His face and follow the ark of His might, power, and glory. He showed them holy reverence for His name and glory. They learned how to worship the Lord through their giving: burnt offerings, grain offerings, fellowship offerings, sin offerings, guilt offerings, freewill offerings, first fruits, and tithing.

Since they had been enslaved for 430 years, they needed to learn how to worship God through giving while they were still on a journey to the Promised Land. True worship always involves giving and receiving. The Lord promised them that through this process as they worshiped Him, He would release His blessings on them. "Worship the Lord your God, and his blessing will be on your food and water. I will take away sickness from among you, and none will miscarry or be barren in your land. I will give you a full life span" (Exodus 23:25–26). What amazing promises! Building the tabernacle, according to God's design, is for the blessing of the people as much as preparing the place for the glory of God to dwell among them to maintain the principle of open heavens.

The Lord wanted worship to be ongoing in order for His presence to abide among them. God dwells in or inhabits the worship and praises of His people. The tabernacle was also to provide a prophetic picture for what is coming. Just as Moses prepared the tabernacle for the glory of God to dwell among them, God the Father prepared a body for Christ to tabernacle among us.

When Christ came into the world, he said:
"Sacrifice and offering you did not desire,
  but a body you prepared for me;
  with burnt offerings and sin offerings you were not pleased.
Then I said, 'Here I am—it is written about me in the scroll—
  I have come to do your will, my God.'"
—Hebrews 10:5–7

With the crucifixion on the cross, Jesus paid the price for our sins and gave us access to come to the throne of grace to worship the Lord in spirit and in truth. That is the reason Jesus, Who was full of grace and truth, came to tabernacle among us. "The Word became flesh and made his dwelling among us. We have seen his glory, the glory of the one and only Son, who came from the Father, full of grace and truth" (John 1:14). Because of the prophetic significance, the Lord warned Moses to build the tabernacle according to what He showed him on the mountain. Even small changes or modifications of the pattern affect the prophetic picture, since God's blueprint is eternal. That is one of the reasons why the Lord prefers that the heavens and earth pass away rather than even the smallest letter of His Word. His Word doesn't return to Him without accomplishing His purpose, so it is a pattern given by Him.

We need to understand the depth and width of working with the divine pattern. What God does is eternal, and this has implications not only for the present but also for future generations. The pattern that hosts His glory should be treated as holy, set apart for a special purpose, not common and ordinary. As such, the glory has to be kept pure, not mixed with human plans or strategies. David, who was a man after God's own heart, summarized this process of receiving the pattern with understanding. "'All this,' David said, 'I have in writing as a result of the LORD's hand on me, and he enabled me to understand all the details of the plan'" (1 Chronicles 28:19).

In this process, we must pay attention to both receiving the right pattern and comprehending the pattern for implementation that comes from the Holy Spirit. Studying the pattern for intellectual analysis is not the point, but rather, like David, waiting upon the Lord for the revelation from the Holy Spirit. The pattern is the truth God gives to us to build upon, so He is able to fill it with His glory. Revelation is the leading of the Holy Spirit, step-by-step, to build according to the pattern without adding to it or trying to modify it for cultural adaptation.

Faithfulness to what we receive from Him qualifies us to build for His glory and the release of the manifestation of His presence. The purpose of the divine pattern is to prepare a place for the ark of His presence to dwell in its fullness. God's pattern is not *one* of the options we can use to build for His glory, because it is the *only* option we are given. Neither is it a matter of opinion, but rather a command that we must obey to stay under open heavens.

In this sense, the call to the Body of Christ today is that as much as we want to run to do the work of ministry, the time has come to run to God and stay in His presence until we receive both the pattern and His revelation about the pattern. This is the way the Spirit of God is moving in this hour. Moses stayed in God's presence on the mountain under the covering of the glory until he received the pattern with instructions from God. David remained before the Lord until he received the revelation of the pattern in detail with understanding.

The challenge today is that we don't have the patience to wait upon the Lord for His pattern and the understanding of His purposes. As a result, we work with patterns we create under the label of short-term and long-term strategic planning goals. They appear to be very impressive, but the questions are, "Where is the glory the Lord wants to reveal through us for the world to see? Where did you find the pattern you have employed in your ministry, business, or profession?"

TABERNACLE: A PLACE OF OPEN HEAVENS

Moses completed, inspected, and approved to confirm that everything was built according to the pattern received from the Lord while he was on the mountain where the glory of God dwelt. The Lord instructed the people to set up the tent of meeting on the first day of the first month: "The LORD spoke to Moses, saying, 'On the first day of the first month (Abib) you shall set up the tabernacle of the tent of meeting [of God with you]'" (Exodus 40:1–2, AMP).

This was a new beginning for God's people. They were about to experience the indwelling of God's presence. They witnessed His deliverance, but after this, they would see His manifested glory to guide, protect, and provide for them daily while under open heavens. When they set up the tabernacle, the Lord was answering Moses's prayer. "If your Presence does not go with us, do not send us up from here" (Exodus 33:15). His presence is what has made the people of God different throughout the years. Jesus came to set us apart by His glorious presence. He brought us the Kingdom of light, and we became children of light to reflect His glory.

According to the Lord's instruction, Moses set up the tabernacle—the tent of meeting—in the middle of the camp, and the 12 tribes surrounded the tabernacle: three on the East, three on the West, three on the North, and three on the South. The Israelites had a full view of the erected tabernacle from four primary directions.

After setting up the tent of meeting, Moses brought Aaron and his sons to the tent of meeting. They were washed and dressed in sacred garments and anointed for consecration to serve the Lord. He organized the furniture according to the pattern from the altar of offering, the washing basin, the table with bread of presence, the lampstand, the golden altar (altar of incense), and the ark of the covenant. He put up the curtains in their appropriate places. Subsequently, Moses took the anointing oil to anoint the tabernacle and everything in it. "Moses did everything just as the LORD commanded Him. . . . And so Moses finished the work" (Exodus 40:16, 33).

TIME FOR THE DWELLING GLORY UNDER OPEN HEAVENS

Then the cloud [the Shekinah, God's visible presence] covered the tent of meeting, and the glory of the LORD filled the tabernacle. Moses could not enter the tent of meeting because the cloud had settled on it, and the glory of the LORD filled the tabernacle.

—Exodus 40:34–35

At the beginning, the Lord told Moses to build the tabernacle according to the pattern, for Him to dwell among His people. At its completion, the Lord came with His visible presence to the tabernacle. Moses spent time with God on the mountain under the glory cloud. In that setting, God gave Moses a pattern to build the tent of meeting, so that He could come and be among His people. Moses obeyed the Lord, and the glory came and filled the tabernacle. The intensity of the glory that filled the tabernacle was much greater than what Moses experienced on the mountain. When the mountain was covered with the cloud of the glory of God for forty days and nights, Moses was on the mountain. But when the Glory filled the tabernacle, Moses was not able to enter it.

When we build according to the pattern, the glory is not only for a few to see. Just as the twelve tribes saw the cloud of the glory of the Lord among them at the tent of meeting, "All people will see it together." Willingness to build what is able to host the glory of His presence is required, but we must receive the blueprint or pattern on the mountain by being in the cloud of His glory. God has a pattern that reveals the glory of His presence today among the Body of Christ for the world to see and experience the demonstration of the power of His glorious presence. Flexibility is caused by revelation, while building right is a result of commitment to the pattern.

God's glorious presence changes the pace of our journey. After the glory filled the tabernacle and the cloud of glory settled on the tent of meeting, their journey that had been familiar was changed.

> In all the travels of the Israelites, whenever the cloud lifted from above the tabernacle, they would set out; but if the cloud did not lift, they did not set out—until the day it lifted. So the cloud of the LORD was over the tabernacle by day, and fire was in the cloud by night, in the sight of all the Israelites during all their travels.
> —Exodus 40:36–38

Now they needed to learn to watch the cloud on their journey, since they were under open heavens. Where the glory of the Lord is, there is divine guidance. God is among His people to protect, provide for, and guide them. These are the key characteristics of a good shepherd.

Following the cloud is a sign of accepting the leadership of the Lord, the Good Shepherd. The other point is to know the Lord's timing. When we follow the cloud of the glory of God, we stay in His timetable, and we do not miss His perfect will. Furthermore, when we follow the cloud of His presence, we live by His agenda—not by ours. There is a total rest in following the cloud of God. True peace is being in His revealed will.

Finally, they followed the cloud of fire. This is about both the leading and the protection of God. The Lord promised Moses to go ahead of them like a devouring fire, to give them victory over their enemies. The point to remember is that walking with God isn't only about guidance, but it is also about fellowship with Him. God created us to walk with Him. He dwells among us, so we can fellowship with Him.

When God asked Moses to build the tabernacle and dwell among them, the people gained access to approach Him in worship and establish a lasting relationship with God, Who had delivered them. This is the true sign of open heavens. They saw the glorious presence of God daily during their journey. In the sight of all the Israelites during their travels, a visible glory was in their midst, drawing them to the Lord for worship. When a person sees the glory of God, all they can do is worship, and lasting transformation takes place. Dwelling in a glory zone of worship, as Moses did, changes a person. The presence of the glory of God saturated Moses's total being, and he ended up reflecting the glory without being aware of it.

The intensity of God's glory increases during true worship, a sign of true transformation. God's plan and desire is to change His people into His likeness by His dwelling presence. His power is to create, save, sustain, heal, restore, protect, provide, and lead, along with revealing His majesty, beauty, greatness, and holiness. Holiness, in context, is the attribute of God that changes us into His likeness because of the intensity of God's glorious presence. Walking in holiness is hosting His presence, and this causes us to become more like Him. The sign of open heavens is THE GLORY OF HIS PRESENCE! And we turn now to the temple as another sign.

Questions for Reflection and Discussion

1. What new information about the tabernacle did you encounter in this chapter?
2. A key statement and theological truth in this chapter is that "Jesus, who was full of grace and truth, came to tabernacle among us." Why is that so central to the Christian message? How does that reality change everything for us?
3. How has God's glorious presence changed the pace of your journey of faith?

CHAPTER 6

THE TEMPLE AS A SIGN OF OPEN HEAVENS

David received the pattern for the temple to leave for his son Solomon. "The whole [is] in writing from the hand of Jehovah, 'He caused me to understand all the work of the pattern,' [said David]" (1 Chronicles 28:19, YLT).

When David heard from Nathan the prophet what the Lord said about building the temple, he was overwhelmed with the Lord's goodness and mercy. He responded to the Lord's message by sitting before God in a spirit of worship, praise, and thankfulness for what the Lord had revealed. After that, he started making extensive preparations before his death for building the temple of God. He organized the builders of God's house to help young Solomon. "You have many workers: stonecutters, masons and carpenters, as well as those skilled in every kind of work in gold and silver, bronze and iron— craftsmen beyond number. Now begin the work, and the LORD be with you" (1 Chronicles 22:15–16).

David also provided for building materials such as gold, silver, and iron to make nails, bronze, and cedar logs. He encouraged and ordered the people and all the leaders of Israel to help Solomon in building the temple and appointed a supervisor of the work. He set apart the priests to consecrate the most holy things, offer sacrifices before the Lord, minister before Him, and pronounce blessings in the name of the Lord forever. He also set apart prophets for the ministry of prophesying with musical instruments and singers (1 Chronicles 25). He put gatekeepers in their places (1 Chronicles 26).

Finally, David charged his son Solomon to build the Lord's house: "Now, my son, the LORD be with you, and may you have success and build the house of the LORD your God, as he said you would." He also blessed his son by saying, "May the LORD give you discretion and understanding when he puts you in command over Israel, so that you may keep the law of the LORD your God" (1 Chronicles 22:11, 12).

BUILD ACCORDING TO THE OPEN HEAVENS PATTERN

The process that brought David to the place where he received the pattern for the temple is very significant. Paying close attention to key issues in the process of what we are building is essential. The first issue was David's desire to build the temple in reverence to the name of the Lord, so the nation would honor the holiness of God and embrace a holy reverence for God. That desire was the reflection of his heart and his motive for honoring God. True love is the source of a pure heart. "The goal of this command is love, which comes from a pure heart and a good conscience and a sincere faith" (1 Timothy 1:5). David oversaw all of the preparatory planning for building the temple.

In addition to making all the preparations, King David went to the Lord to ask for a pattern for building the temple. The Lord wrote with His hand the pattern's detail and gave it to King David. The Spirit of God also gave him an understanding of the necessary details, along with the pattern and specifications of every aspect of the temple. He sought the Lord for a revelation of the pattern and waited upon the Lord to receive the blueprint for understanding for the sake of the next generation. In doing this, David corrected history by bringing back the ark of the presence of God and now shaped the future by receiving the pattern with revelation.

With a pure heart and the right motive, the temple was built to last, as well as to display God's holiness and to keep open heavens over the Israelites. He shows us the pattern for our current time, according to our heart's desire. The passion of our heart is the driving engine of our lives.

David sought the Lord to receive the pattern for his son to build according to God's plan. Many times, we see a pattern and can go as far as identifying both human and financial resources to build it. However, we don't have the patience to wait upon the Lord to receive revelation about the pattern. Consequently, we pass on a formula that has no spirit or life to it. Without revelation, the pattern becomes a lifeless system without any fruit.

David ". . . couldn't build a temple for the name of the LORD our God until the LORD let him defeat his enemies" (1 Kings 5:3, GWT). His calling was to fight and destroy his enemies in order to prepare the way for his son to build the temple in a time of peace. Solomon received not only the pattern but also the godly advice and materials his father provided for building. He started the process according to the pattern David received from the Lord, 480 years after the Israelites had left Egypt. Solomon began building in the fourth year of his reign. "The temple was finished according to all its plans and specifications. He spent seven years building it" (1 Kings 6:38, GWT).

The temple was completed in the seventh year and the seventh month. The ark and other holy utensils were brought from the tent into the temple to complete the process. The tent was a temporary dwelling, while the temple was a permanent, lasting dwelling. The temple was similar to the tabernacle in its setup.

A detailed description of the temple's pattern is found in Ezekiel 40–48 and 1 Kings 5–8. The major differences were the materials and their purposes. The two patterns that were given by the Lord were the reflection of these differences and similarities.

Like the tabernacle, the temple was also built according to the pattern given by God, and it received God's approval in the form of His fire and glory as a sign of open heavens.

> When Solomon finished praying, fire came down from heaven and consumed the burnt offering and the sacrifices, and the glory of the LORD filled the temple. The priests could not enter the temple of the LORD because the glory of the LORD filled it.
> —2 Chronicles 7:1–2

What an awesome sight! The temple was built according to the pattern and was accepted. The prayer was heard, and fire came down to establish God's presence. The glory of the Lord filled the temple, and there was not a place for anyone else in the holy temple, except for God. By sending the fire and filling the temple with His glory, God established a standard for His temple and affirmed the promise of open heavens. The Lord reminded His people about this standard in Ezekiel's vision about the temple of God. In the temple, the Lord displayed His holiness for His people to fear and honor Him. One other time the Israelites saw the glory of the Lord on a mountain like a fire. This was the second time the Lord sent His fire and His glory at the same time.

The tabernacle was built for God to dwell among His people and host His presence. On the other hand, the temple was built for the Lord to dwell in, not only among the tribes, but also in the land, so all who were near and far, all who were present, all in future generations, and the nation of Israel and the Gentiles would see His holiness: "This is the place of my throne and the place for the soles of my feet. This is where I will live among the Israelites forever" (Ezekiel 43:7).

Everything in the temple was to show His holiness, including the pattern of the temple. This is what the Lord told Ezekiel:

> Son of man, describe the temple to the people of Israel, that they may be ashamed of their sins. Let them consider its perfection, and if they are ashamed of all they have done, make known to them the design of the temple—its arrangement, its exits and entrances—its whole design and all its regulations and laws. Write these down before them so that they may be faithful to its design and follow all its regulations.
> —Ezekiel 43:10–11

The message is that receiving the pattern, understanding the pattern, being faithful to the pattern, and passing the pattern to the next generation to build, according to the heavenly design to reflect the holiness of God, is a must to keep open heavens. The temple was built to show the visible presence of God and draw others to come to the house of God. "In the last days the mountain of the LORD's temple will be established as the highest of the mountains; it will be exalted above the hills, and all nations will stream to it" (Isaiah 2:2). The temple of the Lord is the hope of nations, to be seen with all its pattern, design, and laws. The law of the temple is to keep the surrounding area on the top of the mountain most holy. "As a shepherd looks after his scattered flock when he is with them, so will I look after my sheep. I will rescue them from all the places where they were scattered on a day of clouds and darkness" (Ezekiel 34:12).

One of the sins of the people was they did not leave enough space between their things and the holy things of the Lord. "They put their doorway by my doorway and their doorposts by my doorposts. Only a wall separated me from them. They dishonored my holy name because of the disgusting things that they have done" (Ezekiel 43:8, GWT).

This is a common sin among those who serve the Lord. Because of the blessings, favor, and mercy of God, we start to take things for granted. When we first experience the holy presence, anointing, and manifestation of the glory of God, we praise and worship Him. However, if we don't keep that reverence by walking in a pure heart and a clear conscience, soon the familiarity reduces the holy fear of God. At that stage, the boundaries become blurred, and leaders too easily move from stewardship into an ownership attitude. They start feeling that all the success is their own doing, and they are indispensable in the Kingdom work. Once pride starts settling in, they stop listening, refuse correction, resist submission, and ignore advice. King Uzziah started with the fear of the Lord by listening to the prophet Zechariah. But when his fame spread far and wide because of the help and blessing of the Lord, he became unfaithful to the Lord. He refused the voice of 81 priests and entered the temple of God to burn incense on the altar of incense, and he ended up with leprosy. Burning incense on the altar was reserved only for the priests. Some people cross the line, while others remove the boundaries because of pride.

In summary, the pattern of the Lord's temple was given to David to establish a lasting presence of God in Israel and Jerusalem for the experience of living under open heavens. The purpose was to bring change and transformation not only to the faithful worshipers but also to the city, the nation, and all the nations, since His house was to be called the house of prayer for the nations. After the temple of God was built according to the pattern, His glory and fire came down. "From then on the city's name will be: The LORD Is There" (Ezekiel 48:35). This is called the sustainable transformation of a nation and a city.

The pattern of the temple was to bring back God's holiness in tangible ways to individuals, families, communities, cities, and nations for others to magnify, exalt, and glorify His holy name. As it was confirmed through Ezekiel's vision of the temple over and over again, both the building and the restoration of the temple were to establish a permanent presence of God in the land and among the people of God, to declare the holiness of God ("This is the Most Holy Place" [Ezekiel 41:4]), release the fullness of His glory ("I . . . saw the glory of the LORD filling the temple of the LORD" [44:4]), bring the holy fear and reverence of God ("I fell facedown" [44:4]), and establish divine order ("This is the law of the temple" [43:12]). The divine pattern reveals divine order that the generation was able to follow both in understanding and implementation. The pattern was given to David because of his relationship, his life of worship, his commitment to the purpose of God, and his care for the success of the next generation.

The first question for us is whether we have the right pattern to build to show His holiness. The second question is if we have the right heart, motive, and commitment to receive the right pattern, so we can pass it on to the next generation. "This is the law of the temple: As it radiates from the top of the mountain, everything around it becomes holy ground. Yes, this is law, the meaning, of the Temple" (Ezekiel 43:12, MSG).

Questions for Reflection and Discussion

1. Receiving, understanding, being faithful, and passing the pattern to the next generation is a key teaching of this chapter. What does it mean to "build according to the open heavens pattern"?
2. How do we ensure we have the right pattern in our own lives? What are the markers, the signposts?
3. What does it mean to have the "right heart, motive, and commitment" to receive it?

CHAPTER 7

THE PROPHETS AND OPEN HEAVENS

Historically, from the time the Israelites entered the Promised Land as a nation, their primary challenge was to stay under open heavens and enjoy the blessings of God. God's desire and plan was for them to stay under open heavens through their obedience to His laws and enjoy His abundant blessings.

The worship of God under open heavens was the true foundation for all the blessings God had for them. They were receiving God's blessings and had become a blessing to others through true worship. The Lord told them on Mount Sinai that His blessings are released through obedience to His word. "All these blessings will come upon you and accompany you if you obey the LORD your God" (Deuteronomy 28:2). In addition, He sent the Prophet Isaiah to remind them the same thing again by saying, "If you are willing and obedient, you will eat the good things of the land" (Isaiah 1:19).

THE PRIESTS AND OPEN HEAVENS

The desire of God was for the priests to stay under open heavens, for generational blessings. He established a priestly system to relate to the people through ongoing worship. He anointed high priests to pray, bless, and teach them about the world God had prepared, so they could worship the Lord in holiness and purity. The primary call of priests is to stand before God and to minister to Him. During his restoration, King Hezekiah called the priests to their original responsibility highlighted by their true calling: "My sons, do not be negligent now, for the LORD has chosen you to stand before him and serve him, to minister before him and to burn incense" (2 Chronicles 29:11). This is the only way to experience the reality of open heavens.

The first priests who were anointed and set apart to carry out these responsibilities were Aaron and his sons. However, Aaron, the high priest, led the people into idol worship when he made a golden calf before Moses came down from Mount Sinai (Exodus 32:4). Aaron's two sons sinned against God by using unauthorized fire for the altar. All this started even before they entered the Promised Land.

After they entered the Promised Land, built the temple, and settled as a nation, the priests turned away from God. The story about Eli's sons gives us a very clear picture of the priests' hearts. The Bible summarizes the sons of Eli: "Eli's sons were scoundrels; they had no regard for the LORD" (1 Samuel 2:12). They were chosen by God to stand before Him and bring holy sacrifices, teach God's people His ways, and pronounce His blessings. Following that time, the priests' sins continued and finally resulted in God's judgment. The heavens were closed over the nation because they had been apostate. The Prophet Elijah declared, "The Israelites have rejected your covenant, torn down your altars, and put your prophets to death with the sword. I am the only one left, and now they are trying to kill me too" (1 Kings 19:10). The priests were responsible for the altar of God, but they tore it down. Finally, as designated under the closed heavens, the provision of God was taken away, but also the protection of God was removed, and the people were taken into captivity. The temple of God, a sign of open heavens, was destroyed by the enemy.

Following that time throughout the Old Testament, the priests' sins became more wicked—but this also was addressed by the prophets. The Lord raised up prophets, just like Samuel, to bring correction and spiritual restoration. The Prophet Malachi's message highlights the total picture of the attitude of the priests, who were chosen to stand before God to facilitate worship, when the Lord said, "'A son honors his father, and a slave his master. If I am a father, where is the honor due me? If I am a master, where is the respect due me?' says the LORD Almighty. 'It is you priests who show contempt for my name'" (Malachi 1:6). Because of the priests' evil sins, rather than instructing the people to seek God, they violated the covenant, the Lord cursed them, and they missed God's blessings. They were off course, and this closed the heavens over the nation.

"But you are a chosen people, a royal priesthood, a holy nation, God's special possession, that you may declare the praises of him who called you out of darkness into his wonderful light" (1 Peter 2:9). That is living under open heavens!

THE PROPHETS AND OPEN HEAVENS

The Lord started raising up prophets to speak directly to priests who were neglecting their calling and rebelling against God. He raised prophets to call God's people back to stay under open heavens. The first prophet for this assignment was Samuel. As a boy, Samuel gave the first prophetic message that was not for the nation, but for the high priest, Eli. The saddest thing was that Eli didn't repent and seek the face of God. As a result, the glory of God departed from his family and the nation. Closed heavens!

Throughout the Old Testament, the heavens were closed as the people turned to idol worship. The ministry of prophets was to warn and call them back to God's presence and purpose. Elijah was one of the prophets who understood the importance of open and closed heavens. He was called by God and sent to the Israelites during the darkest time in the nation's spiritual condition. Elijah was zealous for the glory of God when his nation turned its back to the Lord by rejecting His covenant, tearing down His altars of worship, and putting His prophets to death with the sword. During that period, Elijah prayed earnestly that it would not rain and for the Lord to keep the heavens closed. The Lord gave him the authority to stop the rain by closing the heavens until the Israelites knew that the sources of their blessings were from God, Who opened the heavens over them. With that authority, Elijah went to King Ahab: "There will be neither dew nor rain in the next few years except at my word" (1 Kings 17:1). The phrase "except at my word" was proof he was given authority by God to close the heavens. It happened just as he declared it! It did not rain on the land for three and a half years. After three and half years, the neglected altar of God was repaired again. Elijah prayed, the heavens gave rain, and the earth produced crops. The hearts of the people turned back to God again.

True worship is the key to opening and closing the heavens. By neglecting the altar of God, the Israelites brought a curse upon themselves. The Old Testament prophets were called and anointed by God to bring back correction through repentance for open heaven blessings. The prophets themselves started their ministry under open heavens by receiving a clear vision from God. Here are some good examples.

- Moses
  "Saw the God of Israel" (Exodus 24:10).

- Ezekiel
  "The heavens were opened and I saw visions of God." "There before me was the glory of the God of Israel, as in the vision I had seen in the plain" (Ezekiel 1:1, 8:4).
- Isaiah
  "I saw the Lord, high and exalted, seated on a throne, and the train of his robe filled the temple" (Isaiah 6:1).
- Daniel
  "In my vision at night I looked, and there before me was one like a son of man, coming with the clouds of heaven. He approached the Ancient of Days and was led into his presence" (Daniel 7:13). Wow! What an open heavens experience.
- Other minor prophets had very similar experiences.

Starting under open heavens and staying under open heavens was the thing that separated true prophets of God from false prophets. What that means is starting in God's presence, hearing His voice, and walking with Him daily by being sensitive to His voice. Among other advantages, open heavens are a sign of God's manifested presence. Because the need for open heavens was great, Isaiah prayed this prayer: "Oh, that you would rip open the heavens and descend, make the mountains shudder at your presence" (Isaiah 64:1, MSG). However, the nation of Israel didn't respond in a true spirit of repentance for a long period of time, nor did they stay under open heavens. Consequently, for 400 years there were closed heavens without the voice and vision of God until the Lord sent the final prophet of the Old Testament, John the Baptist. After a rebuke of the priests for their sin, a promise was given to open the heavens again.

"See, I will send the prophet Elijah to you before that great and dreadful day of the LORD comes. He will turn the hearts of the parents to their children, and the hearts

of the children to their parents; or else I will come and strike the land with total destruction."
—Malachi 4:5–6

Yes, John the Baptist was the last Old Testament prophet who came with a message of repentance that prepared the way for Jesus, who started His earthly ministry under open heavens with the final authority of the key of David. "What he opens no one can shut, and what he shuts no one can open" (Revelation 3:7).

Next, we'll turn to the One whom John the Baptist foreshadowed, as we look at Jesus and the open heavens.

Questions for Reflection and Discussion

1. What was the purpose of God's raising up prophets?
2. What is the distinction between "true prophets" and "false prophets"?
3. Why was John the Baptist's message of repentance so important, and how was it a foreshadowing of Christ's work in the world?

CHAPTER 8

JESUS AND OPEN HEAVENS

When the glory of God was to be revealed for all humanity on earth, John the Baptist came with the anointing of Elijah to preach repentance. John the Baptist preached with a prophetic voice to prepare the way. He came out of the wilderness announcing the arrival of Jesus. This is recorded at the beginning of the New Testament.

The unique elements of John's ministry were his spirit and the core of his message. He came with the spirit of a true prophet to give direction. The prophet Elijah came forward with a strong message that closed and also opened the heavens. The nation of Israel's sins were those of rejecting God's covenant, tearing down God's altars, and putting God's prophets to death with the sword. He prayed for the Lord to close the heavens and stop the rain that were a sign of God's blessings. For three and half years there was no rain in the land. Elijah restored the altar, turning the people's hearts back to God. He brought the voice of the prophet alive again by asking God first for fire and rain that released blessings again.

John the Baptist was sent in the spirit and power of Elijah to turn people's hearts toward God. He prepared the way for the Messiah to open the heavens that had been closed for 400 years. For this to occur, at the beginning of Jesus's ministry, He went to the Jordan and was baptized by John. "As soon as Jesus was baptized, he went up out of the water. At that moment heaven was opened, and he saw the Spirit of God descending like a dove and alighting on him. And a voice from heaven said, 'This is my Son, whom I love; with him I am well pleased'" (Matthew 3:16–17).

The first thing that happened in the ministry of Jesus was the heavens opened up, which meant the curse was broken and a relationship was restored between God and His people. Open heavens are both a sign and an invitation from the Lord for a new beginning with a new level of relationship, revelation, restoration, and recovery. Other signs included a connection between heaven and earth, releasing ministering angels, prophetic visions for the future (Revelation 4:1), and a manifestation of the glory of God (Acts 7).

Open heavens are all about a relationship with our Creator, Redeemer, King, and Counselor. God's invitation from the beginning has been, "Come, turn, and return to me." The core message of the Bible is "come."

- "Come to the water," Isaiah's message
- "Come and live," Ezekiel's message
- "Come and follow me," Jesus's invitation
- "Come and see," Jesus's invitation
- "Come and rest," Jesus's invitation
- "Come and eat," Jesus's invitation
- "Come up here," the Father's invitation

An open heaven is first established for a relationship with God. This is an invitation to the throne room to see the glory of the King and His Kingdom. When Isaiah entered the throne room, he saw the Lord on His throne, high and lifted up. He also saw the Kingdom and the King. "The whole earth is full of his glory."

Revelation also opens up. When we are under an open heaven and in a relationship with the eternal God, we walk in true revelation that God, the Holy Spirit, gives us continually. The nature of the invitation is, "Come up here, and I will show you what must take place after this." When we are under an open heaven we see clearly both what is here now and what is yet to come.

An open heaven is all about restoration. We walk under an open heaven, and the Lord restores to us what the enemy has stolen in the past. "See if I will not throw open the floodgates of heaven and pour out so much blessing that there will not be room enough to store it" (Malachi 3:10). When we are in a right relationship with the King of glory, we walk in the revelation of His Kingdom. It is natural to seek right standing with Him and His Kingdom, and this releases blessings and restores what was lost in the last season.

No wonder Jesus started His ministry under open heavens. When Jesus came out of the water and prayed, the things that followed took place immediately. Because of the opening of the heavens, the Holy Spirit rested upon Him. Jesus was conceived by the Holy Spirit. He was filled with the Holy Spirit, and He was led by the Holy Spirit to defeat Satan in the wilderness.

Jesus, full of the Holy Spirit, left the Jordan and was led by the Spirit into the wilderness, where for forty days he was tempted by the devil. He ate nothing during those days, and at the end of them he was hungry. The devil said to him, "If you are the Son of God, tell this stone to become bread." Jesus answered, "It is written: 'Man shall not live on bread alone.'"

—Luke 4:1–4

First, He was empowered by the Holy Spirit for the call on His life. "Jesus returned to Galilee in the power of the Spirit, and news about him spread through the whole countryside. He was teaching in their synagogues, and everyone praised him. He went to Nazareth, where he had been brought up, and on the Sabbath day he went into the synagogue, as was his custom" (Luke 4:14–16). He stood up and read from Isaiah 61. He was anointed by the Holy Spirit to fulfill the prophetic destiny about His life.

> The Spirit of the Sovereign LORD is on me, because the LORD has anointed me to proclaim good news to the poor. He has sent me to bind up the brokenhearted, to proclaim freedom for the captives and release from darkness for the prisoners, to proclaim the year of the LORD's favor and the day of vengeance of our God, to comfort all who mourn, and provide for those who grieve in Zion—to bestow on them a crown of beauty instead of ashes, the oil of joy instead of mourning, and a garment of praise instead of a spirit of despair. They will be called oaks of righteousness, a planting of the LORD for the display of his splendor.
> —Isaiah 61:1–3

> "The Spirit of the Lord is on me, because he has anointed me to proclaim good news to the poor. He has sent me to proclaim freedom for the prisoners and recovery of sight for the blind, to set the oppressed free, to proclaim the year of the Lord's favor."
> —Luke 4:18–19

Second, the voice of the Father came. The silence of 400 years was broken, and the voice of God was heard by those who came to watch the baptism of the Lord Jesus. God spoke to the people about Jesus by saying that He is His son, He loves Him, and He is well pleased with Him. What a confirmation of the life of the Lord Jesus. It was an awesome way to start ministry based on relationship and love. The New Testament pattern of ministry is a life of testimony. Ministry is a byproduct of a life of obedience in true love and sincere worship and praises.

Jesus started His public ministry under open heavens. The most important thing about open heavens is having access to the throne room of God Almighty despite our circumstances, just like Stephen. "'Look,' he said, 'I see heaven open and the Son of Man standing at the right hand of God'" (Acts 7:56). The testimony of John is very similar. "After this I looked, and there before me was a door standing open in heaven" (Revelation 4:1). He stayed under open heavens every day of his earthly ministry. That is the New Testament pattern.

This is part of a balancing act of walking under open heavens, as well as opening doors and ancient gates for the King of glory to come and establish His ever-increasing Kingdom power and authority, so that every tongue and every tribe would cry out together.

There were loud voices in heaven, which said:

"The Kingdom of the world has become the Kingdom of our Lord and of his Messiah,
     and he will reign for ever and ever."

And the twenty-four elders, who were seated on their thrones before God, fell on their faces and worshiped God, saying:

"We give thanks to you, Lord God Almighty,
          the One who is and who was,
     because you have taken your great power
          and have begun to reign.
The nations were angry,
          and your wrath has come.

The time has come for judging the dead,
    and for rewarding your servants the prophets
and your people who revere your name,
        both great and small—
and for destroying those who destroy the earth."
—Revelation 11:15–18

Questions for Reflection and Discussion

1. What does it mean for the "open heaven to be all about restoration"? How does this bring comfort and hope to your life?
2. Reread the passage about Jesus's baptism by John in the Jordan River. What stands out most vividly for you in that portrait? Why?
3. How do you respond to the vision you see in the Revelation 11:15–18 passage that concludes this chapter?

CHAPTER 9

THE APOSTLES AND OPEN HEAVENS

The death and resurrection of Jesus created the opening of heavens over those who want to come to the Lord permanently. By His death, Jesus removed the curse that hindered the blessings of God's covenant when He paid the price with His crucifixion on a cross. "Cursed is everyone who is hung on a pole" (Galatians 3:13). A curse closes the heavens and separates us from our relationship with our God. The One Who was given the key of David opened the heavens once and for all. What He opens no one can shut. After the resurrection of Jesus, open heavens are for whoever will come.

THE CHURCH AND OPEN HEAVENS

After the Resurrection, Jesus revealed Himself to His disciples through a closed door and declared peace over them by standing in their midst. Yes, what He opens, no one can shut! He showed them His hands and His side as proof of His resurrection and the price He paid for their salvation and calling. Shortly after, He told them that He would send them just as His Father had sent Him, and He breathed into them to receive the Holy Spirit. The heavens were opened! The same

Holy Spirit that came upon them at His water baptism, when the heavens were opened for the first time, was now upon them. They waited in Jerusalem until He asked the Father, and the promised Holy Spirit was sent for the church to be born and function under open heavens.

On the day of Pentecost, God opened the heavens and poured out the promised Holy Spirit, while the disciples were gathering in Jerusalem. "Suddenly a sound like the blowing of a violent wind came from heaven and filled the whole house where they were sitting" (Acts 2:2). Yes, Jesus opened the heavens and poured out the Holy Spirit, Who gave birth to the church that day. It was born with mission and vision. Its mission of prophecy was to declare the truth that the Holy Spirit started that morning. "We hear them declaring the wonders of God in our own tongues!" (Acts 2:11). This is what the Holy Spirit will continue saying to His church until the day she will be taken. "Whoever has ears, let them hear what the Spirit says to the churches" (Revelation 2:7). Her vision is that young men will see visions and her old men will dream dreams to advance the Kingdom light by being witnesses under open heavens.

That day the 120 received the power of the Holy Spirit to be witnesses for the Lord Jesus. Under those open heavens, by the power of the Holy Spirit, Peter stood up with the eleven and declared the good news of the gospel of Jesus Christ. The One Who opened the heavens and sent the promised Holy Spirit came and opened the hearts of those who had rejected Him before. The hearts of 3,000 were opened that day, and they accepted as their Lord and Savior the One they had crucified at Passover, and they were baptized in His name for salvation.

Yes, the Church of Jesus Christ was born under open heavens and started living under an open heaven. Here are some signs of the church under open heavens:

- God's people were filled with the promised Holy Spirit for themselves and for coming generations.
- The church received the power of the Holy Spirit to be a true witness to what they have seen, heard, and experienced.
- God's people received the gifts of the Holy Spirit for the first time in the New Testament.
- They glorified the Lord in their own language.
- They heard the voice of the Holy Spirit.
- They were united in worship.
- God's people became diligent in studying God's Word.
- They fellowshipped together on a regular basis.
- They became diligent in prayer.
- People became generous in giving their resources, their time, and themselves.
- They witnessed for Jesus.
- They walked in great grace.
- They grew in number daily.
- They showed much care for the poor.
- They experienced great favor from God.
- Extraordinary signs and wonders were performed by their hands, and those signs and wonders continued in the lives of ordinary believers.

All these are signs of a healthy church that Jesus promised to build for His glory and the advancement of His Kingdom on earth.

THE APOSTLES AND OPEN HEAVENS

Jesus promised the apostles from the beginning that they would have an open heavens experience. "Very truly I tell you, you shall see 'heaven open, and the angels of God ascending and descending on' the Son of Man" (John 1:51). During His earthly ministry time, He took Peter, James, and John to the mountain of transfiguration, and they saw Jesus in His glory, under open heavens, along with Moses and Elisha. On that mountain, while Peter was talking, the glory cloud enveloped them, and they heard the voice of Father God that was similar to the voice at the water baptism of Jesus: "This is my Son, whom I love; with him I am well pleased. Listen to him!" (Matthew 17:5). The only difference this time is that God the Father gave a command to listen to His son, Jesus. In other words, the Father declared the full authority and majesty of Jesus under open heavens within hearing of the apostles. Peter described the experience of the onlookers: "We were eyewitnesses of his majesty. . . . We ourselves heard this voice that came from heaven when we were with him on the sacred mountain" (2 Peter 1:16, 18). The apostles followed Jesus and validated the open heavens occurrence.

After the day of Pentecost, the apostles continued their ministry under open heavens. Because of open heavens, the Lord himself, who opens them, was involved with the apostles and confirmed His Word with signs and wonders. As the result of open heavens, extraordinary signs and wonders were performed by their hands—to the extent that the sick were healed and delivered by Peter's shadow and Paul's handkerchiefs. The key to all of this was God's presence. Jesus said, "As the Father has sent me, I am sending you" (John 20:21). They started operating under the heavens that He had opened. Open heavens for the apostles consisted of walking with the Lord and dwelling in His presence. He was working with them by confirming His Word with signs and wonders, and this was a sign of confirmation of open heavens (Mark 16:20). They experienced the final opening of the heavens on the Day of Pentecost, both as individuals and as a team, and it continued throughout the New Testament.

STEPHEN AND OPEN HEAVENS

After the Day of Pentecost, when the mighty wind blew and what looked like fiery tongues rested upon them, Stephen was the first person who experienced open heavens in an authentic way. When those who opposed him had falsely accused him, they saw his face shining like an angel. "All who were sitting in the Sanhedrin looked intently at Stephen, and they saw that his face was like the face of an angel" (Acts 6:15). However, that didn't make them stop accusing him falsely. He continued sharing the word, while the Sanhedrin was trying to stone him. They were shaking their fists and gnashing their teeth.

> Stephen, full of the Holy Spirit, looked up to heaven and saw the glory of God, and Jesus standing at the right hand of God.
> —Acts 7:55

> "Look," he said, "I see Heaven open and the Son of Man standing at the right hand of God."
> —Acts 7:56

What a contrast! I haven't seen clearer Scriptures about open heavens than these verses. Open heavens for prophets and apostles were authentic. This is one of the basic foundations for the Lord wanting His body to be built on the teaching of the apostles and prophets.

THE APOSTLE PAUL AND OPEN HEAVENS

Just like the twelve disciples, Paul started under open heavens. Although he called himself the least apostle, he had an amazing experience under open heavens. Jesus Christ revealed himself to Paul and asked him the question that transformed his life: "As he [Paul, then called Saul] neared Damascus on his journey, suddenly a light from heaven flashed around him. He fell to the ground and heard a voice say to him, 'Saul, Saul, why do you persecute me?'" (Acts 9:3–4). Saul had never had a personal encounter with Jesus Christ until that day, when suddenly the heavens were opened over him, and the voice of the Lord came to him. Saul didn't know the Lord's plan for him. God's design for Saul gave him a new name—Paul—and resulted in his becoming one of the most influential New Testament apostles in the chronicles of church history—a purpose ordained long before his birth. The fulfillment of this plan, however, called for an intimate, personal encounter with the Lord Jesus Himself under open heavens. In a very short time under open heavens, Paul's life turned around.

Paul's first question under open heavens was, "Who are you, Lord?" (Acts 9:5). Here he expresses his desire to better know the One Who had just revealed His identity in such a profound way.

Recognizing and establishing the Lordship of Christ is the first step toward a lasting personal transformation for anybody who desires to honor God. Accepting and embracing His Lordship shows that the eyes of our heart see Him and know Him.

The unusual Damascus Road experience introduced Paul to the supreme authority, of which he had been previously unaware. For him to change his ways and obey the Lord, Paul needed to know Christ. He answered Paul's first question, "Who are You?" with two statements. The first was, "I am Jesus." Jesus wanted Paul to know His nature, so He revealed Himself as Messiah, Christ the anointed King and Savior. In essence, He was saying, "I'm the risen Lord, the One you have been denying and trying to stop from being preached." This encounter brought Paul face-to-face with the reality of Christ and His existence. By saying yes to the revealed One, Paul accepted His Lordship, His saving grace, and His subsequent divine authority for true spiritual life.

After his compelling encounter, Paul fully committed himself to Christ and His purposes. He lived a life of uncompromising obedience to his Master. As we study the account of Paul's life and ministry, we discover that he based his life and actions on the truth that he was not his own, but he had been received under open heavens, through his personal encounter with Christ.

The second part of Jesus's answer to Paul's question, "Who are you?" was ". . . whom you are persecuting." This must have been a shocking statement for Paul to hear. Now he was hearing Jesus identify Himself with the very people Paul was seeking to annihilate and destroy—in the name of religion. Jesus stood in defense of His own. In essence, He was saying, "When you persecute them, you persecute Me." He revealed Himself as savior and defender of His own, one of them.

On one occasion, Paul boldly addressed King Agrippa in his own defense concerning a matter. "I was not disobedient to the vision from heaven" (Acts 26:19). A personal encounter and revelation of Christ instilled boldness deep within the heart of the apostles. Meeting the King of kings personally and learning of His authority enabled Paul to address earthly authority. His encounter under open heavens created in him true humility and a necessary conviction to carry the name of Jesus and declare the gospel of the Kingdom with the supernatural power of the Holy Spirit.

As stated in Acts 22:10, Paul's second question to the Lord was, "What shall I do, Lord?" This question addressed his calling and assignment. Jesus had graciously answered Paul's initial question immediately and directly, but this did not prove to be the case with this query. Instead of answering Paul directly, Jesus replied, "Now get up and go into the city, and you will be told what you must do" (Acts 9:6). Paul's first lesson, under open heavens, was accepting the leadership of Jesus and submitting to other brothers and leaders. In other words, Paul's destiny as one of God's chosen apostles, who would be instrumental in helping lay the foundation for the New Testament church, began with a lesson in godly submission.

After being led to Damascus by the men who accompanied him on the road, Paul waited three days, fasting and praying, before a brother came, prayed for him, and revealed God's plan for his life. Under open heavens, now his physical eyes and his spiritual eyes and mind were opened to fulfill his calling of carrying the name of Jesus. He was filled with Holy Spirit. Paul made reference to this truth.

> My message and my preaching were not with wise and persuasive words, but with a demonstration of the Spirit's power, so that your faith might not rest on human wisdom, but on God's power.
> —1 Corinthians 2:4–5

On numerous occasions, Paul wrote about the miracle-working power of the Holy Spirit. Signs, wonders, and miracles were a key component of the New Testament apostles' ministry. He wrote to the church, "I persevered in demonstrating among you the marks of a true apostle, including signs, wonders and miracles" (2 Corinthians 12:12).

Paul received new vision

Ananias went and prayed for Saul to regain his sight. The result: "Immediately, something like scales fell from Saul's eyes, and he could see again" (Acts 9:18). God used Ananias to pray for the restoration of Saul's sight, but the implications of his healing went much deeper. Not only was Saul's physical sight restored, but also his spiritual eyes were opened to see his life from God's perspective.

Paul received specific direction for his life and calling

With Holy Spirit guidance, Ananias told Paul by the Holy Spirit that he was chosen by God to know His will, to see the Righteous One, to hear His voice, and to be a witness, as he would be carrying the name of the Lord. In summary, open heavens gave Paul a personal encounter with Jesus Christ. When we have an experience like Paul's, we know His will, we see Him in light of Who He truly is, and we hear His voice leading us as we lead others into the fullness of His eternal purposes.

Yes, Paul started under open heavens and continued his ministry for years under open heavens. In addition to his regular walk with God, he had a very special experience, a vision of open heavens. Paul stated, "I will go on to visions and revelations from the Lord. . . . [I] was caught up to paradise and heard inexpressible things, things that no one is permitted to tell" (2 Corinthians 12:1, 4). What a revelation! This is what made Paul so extraordinary and his ministry so effective in the Kingdom work. "God did extraordinary miracles through Paul, so that even handkerchiefs and aprons that had touched him were taken to the sick, and their illnesses were cured and the evil spirits left them" (Acts 19:11–12).

THE APOSTLE JOHN AND OPEN HEAVENS

The Apostle John was one of the last apostles who talked about open heavens. He highlights his amazing experiences under open heavens in the Book of Revelation. In Revelation, chapter one, he shared his encounter with the Lord Jesus under open heavens. Some of the most important truths about being under open heavens include these:

First, hearing the voice of God:

- "I heard behind me a loud voice like a trumpet" (Revelation 1:10).
- Jacob heard the voice of the God of Abraham under open heavens (Genesis 32:12).
- The Lord Jesus heard the voice of the Father under open heavens during His water baptism (Mark 9:7).
- The Apostles Peter, James, and John heard the voice of the Father on the Mount of Transfiguration, 'While he was still speaking, a bright cloud covered them, and a voice from the cloud said, 'This is my Son, whom I love; with him I am well pleased. Listen to him!'" (Matthew 17:5).
- Open heavens are for both the prophets and apostles to hear the voice of God.

Second, seeing Jesus in the Middle:

- "Among the lampstands was someone 'like a son of man'" (Revelation 1:13).
- John saw Jesus with His full glory in the center of the seven churches. Yes, He is the head of His church, the builder of His church, and now He is in the middle of His churches.
- Open heavens are to reveal the centrality of Christ in our lives, family, ministry, profession, and business.

Third, understanding His majesty and holiness:

- "His face was like the sun shining in all its brilliance" (Revelation 1:16).
- Open heavens are for us to hear, see, and understand the overwhelming greatness of our God and to fall at His feet with sincere and true worship of heart and attitude.

Fourth, experience His special touch:

- "He placed his right hand on me" (Revelation 1:17). What an experience for the Apostle John, who walked with Jesus during His earthly ministry and witnessed His Resurrection power.

Open heavens are an invitation that says, "I still have more to reveal, and I want to take you higher than where you have been."

What was the reason John, after all these things, heard the calling under open heavens, "The voice I had first heard speaking to me like a trumpet said, 'Come up here, and I will show you what must take place after this'" (Revelation 4:1)?

In spite of our circumstances, we should be under open heavens daily to hear that calling, "Come higher!"

Questions for Reflection and Discussion

1. Christ's death and resurrection are the hinge moment of history that "opens heavens for whoever will come." What hope, joy, or reassurance does this bring to you today?

2. The Day of Pentecost is another hinge moment in this narrative. Why was that day important to the Early Church, and for the church even today?

3. What about Paul's story stands out most dramatically to you? Why?

PART II

WHEN HE *Opens* DOORS AND GATES

CHAPTER 10

OPEN GATES

Open Gates are more about our role as the ambassadors of the King of glory in His Kingdom. Through open heavens, we hear His voice. Through open doors, we do His will on earth. Through open gates, we invite the King of glory into our lives. He opens the heavens and doors of opportunities, so we are able to open the gate for our King.

The King doesn't open a gate for Himself, but trusted, loyal subjects or servants are given the keys of authority to open them for Him. In the New Testament, the Lord Jesus Christ, the King of glory, declared that He gave us the keys of the Kingdom, as well as making us sons and daughters to be co-heirs with Him. That is royal priesthood and kings with the Kingdom authority as a chosen race.

For us sons and daughters of the King, opening the gates for the Lord of lords and King of glory ushers in the fullness of His glorious purpose. It declares that His victory overpowers principalities and nations. "The One who breaks open the way will go up before them; they will break through the gate and go out. Their king will pass through before them, the LORD at their head" (Micah 2:13). His victory is our victory. His children—His church, the called-out legislative body and bride of the King—are His army who will conquer. As His body, we are given full authority to open and close. "Truly I tell you, whatever you bind on earth will be bound in heaven, and whatever you loose on earth will be loosed in heaven" (Matthew 18:18). There is no greater authority than this, since it includes both heaven and earth.

From the beginning, the Lord was looking for individuals, as well as generations, who would do His will on earth by walking under open heavens to open the gates of society for the King of glory. When He found David, an individual, He had him anointed so that he would serve His purpose on earth among his generation while he dwelt in God's presence under an open heaven through worship. In the Spirit David saw the generation the Lord was looking for and declared, "Such is the generation of those who seek him, who seek your face, God of Jacob" (Psalm 24:6).

The primary responsibility of this generation is for Kingdom work to become a reality by balancing actions among open heavens, open doors, and open gates. God is looking for a generation who lives under an open heaven and walks through open doors and opens gates for the King of glory. This is ushering in the presence of God and the authority of Jesus, not only as the Savior, but also as the King of glory.

Lift up your gates, O ye princes, and be ye lifted up, O eternal gates: and the King of Glory shall enter in. Who is this King of Glory? the Lord who is strong and mighty: the Lord mighty in battle. Lift up your gates, O ye princes, and be ye lifted up, O eternal gates: and the King of Glory shall enter in. Who is this King of Glory? . . . the Lord of hosts, he is the King of Glory.
—Psalm 24:7–10, DRA

This is the generation the Lord set apart with prophetic destiny to correct wrong history: a generation to make history by establishing a new, balanced foundation that will shape the future for the next generation by opening the gate for the King of glory. The balance between the Shepherd and the King gives the Body of Christ a greater understanding of the Kingdom of God and His original purpose. Balancing among open heavens (relationships), open doors (ministries), and open gates (authority and victory) will enable this generation to gather a greater, last-day harvest of souls by ushering in the glory of God for the sustainable transformation of society at large to prepare the bride for the Lord Jesus, and for the nations to see her beauty and His greater glory so that "At the name of Jesus every knee should bow, of things in heaven, and things in earth, and things under the earth; and that every tongue should confess that Jesus Christ is Lord, to the glory of God the Father" (Philippians 2:10–11).

The New Testament pattern is heaven-originated. This pattern started when the Word became flesh, dwelt among us, and revealed His glory on earth through His priestly, prophetic, and kingly offices. The first part of the Kingdom pattern requires understanding the incarnation of Jesus's life, and following His life, relationships, and ministries on earth. The second part is the revelation of open heavens, which is about connecting open heavens with earth, to make operational on earth the pattern that has been established in the heavens. For this reason, the Lord Jesus did only what He saw the Father doing in heaven and on earth. Paul confirmed the same thing: "I have received of the Lord that which also I delivered unto you" (1 Corinthians 11:23), and also, "For I neither received it of man, neither was I taught it, but by the revelation of Jesus Christ" (Galatians 1:12).

The focus of this pattern is to make the Kingdom of God a reality on earth by staying under open heavens, maximizing the opportunities and walking through open doors by ushering into every segment of society the presence of the King of glory, the power of the resurrection, Holy Spirit, and revelation and authority from the Word of God.

The effectiveness of the Kingdom pattern requires balancing between the humanity and the divinity of Jesus Christ, between open heavens and open doors, between Good Shepherd and King of glory, between relationship and ministry, between sonship and humble servant.

Open gates are about protecting the safety, security, honor, and resources of the King and the Kingdom. Cities were protected because the king's palace required protection. Building walls and securing gates are all about security and protection for the king, the king's honor, the king's treasure, the king's subjects, and so forth. Securing the wall's gates keeps what is inside safe and keeps out what doesn't belong inside the walls. Restoring or rebuilding the wall is about security and protection for the dignity and glory of the King and the Kingdom's safety. That is what making new history is about. New history can only be secured from the enemy's destruction by guarding what has been corrected from the past. Both repairing the altar and rebuilding the temple aren't effective until we can keep out the enemy. That is the purpose of restoring broken walls.

Since walls are about protection, we build or restore walls to provide fortification and protection for the worship of the King of glory, Jesus Christ. Therefore, spiritual restoration isn't complete until a wall of protection is positioned and in place to the honor of our King.

The story of Nehemiah is a great example for this eternal truth. Nehemiah was the man God called to return to Jerusalem and rebuild the wall around the temple and the city of the King. The name *Nehemiah* means *the Lord comforts*. Nehemiah returned from Babylon with a powerful leadership vision. After the temple's completion, the Lord showed the leaders another dominion that needed restoration for a lasting transformation. That was rebuilding the wall. This is where Nehemiah came in.

As I have mentioned earlier, in ancient times a wall was a fortification for protection and defense for a city or a nation.

It was meant to keep enemies out and people and things safely within. It was also a symbol of security and safety. A wall encircling a city gave a message to their enemies: we are under protection; you cannot harm us. Invaders had to figure out how to deal with city walls in order to get inside. The Babylonians had laid siege to Jerusalem for many years before they broke down the walls that protected the city. When that was accomplished, Jerusalem was unprotected and vulnerable, and that vulnerability brought shame to the people and their king.

While still in captivity, Nehemiah had heard about those who survived the exile and their dire situation because of the broken wall around Jerusalem. The problems were twofold.

First, the gates of Jerusalem were burned down. Gates and walls together mark the boundary between outside and inside. But as a point of entry to a city, a gate is the most important. When the gate is strong and closed, there is no access and no fear of the enemy. If gates aren't strong and closed securely, the wall becomes ineffective. That was the reason Nehemiah wept when he heard reports about the destruction of Jerusalem's gates by fire. He understood the significance of the gates for the protection of the city, the temple, and God's people.

Second, the wall of Jerusalem was broken down. It was a time of great trouble and disgrace for the people despite the restoration of the altar and the temple. Protection was needed for what had been restored. The process of repairing a broken wall is more than physically putting stones in place. The process is more of a spiritual requirement than a physical one. God is the real protector—not strong walls or watchmen. "Unless the LORD watches over the city, the guards stand watch in vain" (Psalm 127:1).

The foundation of rebuilding the wall for protection is spiritual renewal. Spiritual renewal brings back the presence of God, our true protection. Building walls and restoring gates requires an understanding of reality in order to bring about needed change. Nehemiah asked his brother Hanani and other men who came to Jerusalem about the city's condition. He questioned them in order to get firsthand information. If we don't hear right, we can't go forward correctly. Usually, hearing is what leads to action. "When I heard these things, I sat down and wept. For some days I mourned and fasted and prayed before the God of heaven" (Nehemiah 1:4).

The root cause for lacking protection is spiritual. Why did Nehemiah weep when he heard about the condition of Jerusalem? He knew what caused the destruction of the walls.

> I confess the sins we Israelites, including myself and my
> father's family, have committed against you. We have
> acted very wickedly toward you. We have not obeyed
> the commands, decrees and laws you gave your servant
> Moses.
> —Nehemiah 1:6b–7

Restoration of the wall began by recognizing and acknowledging to God the broken spiritual condition of the individuals, families, churches, and cities, and the nation as a whole.

Though he was far away, Nehemiah's genuine heart concern was for the city of God, Jerusalem. His sadness didn't make him hopeless, however. Rather, his sadness caused him to look for hope from the Lord on behalf of his nation. The basis for his hope was God's promises. After he mourned, fasted, and prayed, he reminded the Lord about the covenant He had made with His people. The covenant was being restored through repentance.

> If you return to me and obey my commands, then even
> if your exiled people are at the farthest horizon, I will
> gather them from there and bring them to the place I have
> chosen as a dwelling for my Name.
> —Nehemiah 1:9

That was the day the true rebuilding of the broken wall started. The Lord heard Nehemiah's prayer, and His hand and favor came upon him. This created faith and confidence in Nehemiah to start planning for his journey. The foundation of ever-increasing faith is the Word of God. His presence brings confidence and boldness in our calling in spite of opposition and challenges—all for the promise and the call. "Lift up your heads, you gates; be lifted up, you ancient doors, that the King of glory may come in" (Psalm 24:7).

True spiritual success is the result of God's favor. The favor of God is the fruit of His presence, opening the gate for the King of glory to come in. God's presence is what brings desired results that enable us to rebuild the broken walls in our settings. Nehemiah had been the cupbearer to the Persian King Artaxerxes. He had experience and knowledge, and he was a good manager. Yet, he sought the Lord's favor in preparation for rebuilding the wall. As long as we seek the Lord and learn to depend upon Him, success is granted in spite of the opposition or challenges we might face in the process. This is recorded elsewhere in the Bible. In the life of David, opposition came from Saul.

> [Saul] sent David away from him and gave him command over a thousand men, and David led the troops in their campaigns. In everything he did he had great success, because the LORD was with him.
> —1 Samuel 18:13–14

It is recorded in the life of King Uzziah, who was only age 16 when he was made king, after his father's assassination,

> He sought God during the days of Zechariah, who instructed him in the fear of God. As long as he sought the LORD, God gave him success.
> —2 Chronicles 26:5

Nehemiah embraced the responsibility for the sins in his nation and repented before the Lord, standing in the gap for his nation and the city of God. When we accept responsibility, rather than blaming others, the Lord uses us to bring a solution. The most effective way of opening the gate for the King of Glory is to stand in the gap. The Lord is looking for people who will stand in the gap.

True spirituality involves moving into an extraordinary relationship with the King by opening the door and inviting Him in. This is what great determination is all about. We can make a difference by paying the price for the cause of Christ through total obedience to live for the pleasure and purpose of the King. This calling is not only to open the gate for the King of Glory but also to protect the gate from others coming in. Ezekiel highlighted this important truth in the vision of the temple: "The LORD said to me, 'This gate is to remain shut. It must not be opened; no one may enter through it. It is to remain shut because the LORD, the God of Israel, has entered through it'" (Ezekiel 44:2).

This is the reason why as the Church we are given the keys of the Kingdom, not only to open it for the King of Glory to come in, but also to close it in order to protect the glory of the King. Yes, whatever we open on earth is opened in heaven. Whatever we close on earth will be closed in heaven. This is part of our calling. With His calling, God gives abundant grace, wisdom, and discernment.

First, grace releases God's favor to stand before the King of glory and do His will. Without the favor of God, no one would be able to stand in His presence and serve the Lord's purpose.

Second, grace gives us favor in the eyes of other people— people we need assistance from, people we will work with, people we lead or serve. The key access to God's favor is prayer. Through prayer, we express our total dependence upon the

Lord, we worship and honor Him, and we acknowledge His ability to do in us and through us what He has promised when He comes in. Therefore, the foundation for restoration is to seek God's presence and His hand to make the impossible possible and the unthinkable a reality.

Yes, Nehemiah had a burning within for the restoration of the wall, but he also had clear vision with a practical, sound strategy to rebuild it. Having a burden for the house of God is the starting point, but without clear vision and sound strategy, we can't bring about the desired restoration. Having a solid and sound strategy, vision, passion, management skills, preparation, and an evaluation procedure in place is part of an effective restoration blueprint. All the fivefold ministries are needed to work together to bring about lasting transformation in the Kingdom of God today. The premier call of the fivefold is to open the gate. The gate is for the King of glory to come into churches, cities, regions, and nations.

Apostles are given authority to open gates for cities and regions because they see, know, and are sent by the King, Jesus Christ. Apostolic leaders bring sound strategy and commitment to a process and method to build well. Apostles' core strengths are reasoning and persistence, a clear purpose, and authority to build on a solid foundation. Apostles develop and use networks to benefit the big picture. Every church, ministry, and business needs this kind of leader to fulfill their purpose by ushering in the King of glory as opening cities and regions.

Prophets are given a mandate to open the gate because of the timing and revelation they receive from the Lord (John 8:26–28). Prophets have a strong, value-based vision that focuses on clear goals with identifiable paradigms. They are great leaders because of their sensitivity to the Holy Spirit's leading, as well as their gift to discern trends and see what is coming and open the gate for the King of glory. These leaders are eyes for ministries, churches, and business organizations.

Evangelists are appointed to open both the gates of the cities and human hearts because of the power of the gospel that they are entrusted with, and their love and passion for the lost. Evangelists are driven with great fire and passion for the cause. They enthusiastically advocate for a cause they believe in. They bring life, hope, and excitement to churches, ministries, and businesses by opening eyes to the truth of the gospel. They are salespeople, public relations specialists, and marketing staff. These leaders are personable and good communicators, and they create a desire to be with the King.

Pastors are set apart to open the gates of the cities and their churches because of their love for the people of God. Pastoral leaders offer big, deep-caring hearts for the well-being of people. They have a great sense of responsibilityfor the resources they are entrusted with. They are protectors of human and materialw resources. They are needed and respected because of their caring attitude and commitment to shepherding open hearts to host the King.

Teachers are called to open the gate for the King because of their given revelation from God. They are highly motivated to equip through discipling, edifying and encouraging, training and correcting toward perfection. They are greatly needed for excellence, improvement, and capacity building for ministries, churches, and businesses. They are evaluators, trainers, and human resource managers. They are gifted in making complex ideas easy to understand and practical to execute in opening the gate for the King of glory.

Questions for Reflection and Discussion

1. We can be "sons and daughters of the King"! As you contemplate that truth, how do you receive it? What does that status mean to you?

2. How do you respond to the exhortation that "the primary responsibility of this generation is for Kingdom work to become a reality"?

3. What stands out to you from the teaching of the "fivefold ministries" noted in this chapter? How have you seen the work of apostles, prophets, evangelists, pastors, and teachers in your own context?

CHAPTER 11

OPEN DOORS

O pen doors are about our calling, our life assignment, our opportunities, and the everlasting access that God gives with His special favor to fulfill His purposes on earth. When we walk under open heavens, by staying in the will of the Lord we hear the voice of the King and obey Him. His voice is to give us authority, so that we can be sent by Him to do His will. He gives us open doors to do His work. "See, I have placed before you an open door that no one can shut" (Revelation 3:8). With open doors, the Lord gives special favor, power, and ministry responsibilities. As long as we stay under an open heaven, the Lord is the One Who opens doors and sends us to fulfill our prophetic destiny.

Open doors are the time and the opportunities a person is given to fulfill what they are created for or the purpose of their life. Redeeming the time is maximizing opportunities or walking through open doors to accomplish our goals. In other words, when opportunities present themselves to do things, we have a season or time of open doors. A missed opportunity means the door that was once open is now closed. What was possible before is no longer possible. In the parable of the five wise and the five foolish virgins, Jesus explained this concept wonderfully:

At that time the kingdom of heaven will be like ten virgins who took their lamps and went out to meet the bridegroom. Five of them were foolish and five were wise. The foolish ones took their lamps but did not take any oil with them. The wise, however, took oil in jars along with their lamps. The bridegroom was a long time in coming, and they all became drowsy and fell asleep. At midnight the cry rang out: "Here's the bridegroom! Come out to meet him!" Then all the virgins woke up and trimmed their lamps. The foolish ones said to the wise, "Give us some of your oil; our lamps are going out."

"No," they replied, "there may not be enough for both us and you. Instead, go to those who sell oil and buy some for yourselves." But while they were on their way to buy the oil, the bridegroom arrived. The virgins who were ready went in with him to the wedding banquet. And the door was shut. Later the others also came.

"Lord, Lord," they said. "Open the door for us!" But he replied, "Truly I tell you, I don't know you."

Therefore, keep watch, because you do not know the day or the hour.

—Matthew 25:1–13

In this parable, all ten were given the same opportunity and time. They were given an open door. They were in the same place. But the difference was the wise virgins used their time to buy enough oil for their lamps. However, the foolish virgins didn't use their time or maximize the opportunity they were given to get ready for what was coming. When they went to buy oil for their lamps, the bridegroom arrived. The wise went into the wedding banquet with the bridegroom, and the door was shut. When the foolish came and asked to have the door opened, the answer was, "Truly I tell you, I don't know you." Once the door is closed, the opportunity is gone—forever in most cases. If we don't use it wisely, what is open will be closed, and we will be called foolish because of the missed opportunity.

Another great example about opening and closing is the journey of the Israelites to the Promised Land. The Lord told Abraham, His friend, about the door He would open to freedom for his descendants after 400 years of enslavement. The opportune time arrived, and God brought them out with great signs and wonders. He divided the Red Sea. In the wilderness, they decided to send spies to check out the Promised Land. After they came out from Egypt with the mighty hand of God, rather than entering into the Promised Land by faith, they wanted to gather more evidence about the land. What they forgot was that faith doesn't come through collecting physical evidence, but by hearing the Word of God and believing it.

They sent 12 leaders to spy on the land. The 12 spies came back with undeniable evidence about the promise of God. "We went into the land to which you sent us, and it does flow with milk and honey! Here is its fruit. But the people who live there are powerful, and the cities are fortified and very large" (Numbers 13:27–28). Ten of the spies refused to go into the Promised Land because of fear and unbelief. In other words, they refused to go through the open door by using the opportunity they were given. The door that was open for 40 days was closed for 40 years because of their refusal to go through the open door. Instead of enjoying the land that flowed with milk and honey, they died in the wilderness. The door was shut.

Yes, He has the Key of David, and what He shuts no one can open, and what He opens no one can shut. That is one of the reasons why we should know the right time and season to act accordingly. "From Issachar, men who understood the times and knew what Israel should do" (1 Chronicles 12:30). Because of their knowledge, the men of Issachar helped the Israelites take appropriate action to go through the open doors for that season.

Opening is about discerning the Lord's time and responding to His calling both for eternal life and our prophetic destiny. The Apostle Paul highlighted this very important truth by quoting the Prophet Isaiah in his letter to the church in Corinth.

As God's co-workers we urge you not to receive God's grace in vain. For he says, "In the time of my favor I heard you, and in the day of salvation I helped you." I tell you, now is the time of God's favor, now is the day of salvation.
—2 Corinthians 6:1–2

Paul was urging the Corinthians not to waste the grace that had been released for their salvation. Human beings can't have a relationship with a Holy God without God's grace. The grace of God, the undeserved favor and gift of God, makes for us the impossible possible and the inaccessible accessible. That is walking through the open door Jesus provides. Jesus took the concept of opening doors to its highest level when He said He is the door. God opens the door of salvation and redemption by His grace. For a sinner, accepting God's grace is the entry point into the salvation God provided through the death and resurrection of His son, Jesus Christ. As it is written, "It is by grace you have been saved, through faith—and this not from yourselves, it is the gift of God—not by works, so that no one can boast" (Ephesians 2:8-9). In other words, Paul was asking the Corinthians to maximize the opportunity by using the open door for the day of salvation before the door would be closed.

The Apostle Paul presented the same concept to the church in Ephesus by encouraging them to make the most of every opportunity by redeeming the time. In this context, open doors are a special time the Lord gives us to carry out His will and purpose. This is such a valuable, crucial time or season that we can't afford to waste it, but to redeem it. The idea of redeeming is to recover, buy back, ransom, or rescue from loss or to improve opportunity. It is referred to in the Greek language as *kairos*; the right, critical, or opportune moment or a proper or opportune time for action during an open door.

In Ephesians 5, Paul provides specific things that would help us to redeem our time. First is spiritual awakening. "Wake up, sleeper" (v. 14) to walk in the light of Christ to see, discern, and live a life of resurrection to have power and determination.

Second is living according to the wisdom of God. "Be very careful, then, how you live—not as unwise but as wise" (v. 15). The wisdom of God enables us to make the most of every opportunity, even the negative ones. Because we know when we are in God's timing to do His will in love, everything will work out for our good.

Third is knowing the will of God for the specific time and specific situation to make it work for good and His glory—the key for an open door to do God's will on earth, as it is in heaven.

Fourth is yielding to the Holy Spirit's power. "Instead, be filled with the Spirit" (v. 18). When we surrender to the Holy Spirit, He fills us, He leads us, He empowers and anoints us not only to redeem our time but also to have a lasting impact on our generation just as the Lord Jesus did. "How God anointed Jesus of Nazareth with the Holy Spirit and power, and how he went around doing good and healing all who were under the power of the devil, because God was with him" (Acts 10:38). When Jesus defeated the enemy's temptation, walked in power, preached the good news to the poor, healed the brokenhearted, delivered those who were oppressed by the enemy, released the prisoners, and declared the favorable year of the Lord, that was a change of season.

Fifth is edifying others and glorifying the Lord. "Speaking to one another with psalms, hymns, and songs from the Spirit.

Sing and make music from your heart to the Lord, always giving thanks to God the Father for everything, in the name of our Lord Jesus Christ" (Ephesians 5:19-20). The open door or special time is given to edify and build up others, while we bring sacrifices of praise to the Lord in the spirit of true and sincere worship. In fact, the premier reason for open doors is to accomplish these two things. The first step in being a blessing to others is to be thankful to God in everything and for every blessing. An open door to be a blessing to another person is a special gift from the Lord. That is how we redeem the time: by doing His perfect will.

The sign of spiritual maturity is hearing the voice of the Good Shepherd and opening our door for Him. The spiritual blessing of the church in the Kingdom of God depends on her willingness to open for Him. Revelation from Jesus Christ was released to the church in Laodicea.

"Here I am! I stand at the door and knock. If anyone hears my voice and opens the door, I will come in and eat with that person, and they with me."
—Revelation 3:20

The Lord knocks on the door of every heart through His voice and the Holy Spirit. God's warning is, "So, as the Holy Spirit says: 'Today, if you hear his voice, do not harden your hearts as you did in the rebellion, during the time of testing in the wilderness'" (Hebrews 3:7-8). Refusing to hear His voice or rebelling against His voice is refusing to open the door for the One Who loves us with an unmeasurable love. If we decide to close the door of salvation and redemption, it is for eternity.

Open doors are the opportunities God gives us because of open heavens over us. Open doors are a result of God's favor because of the purpose of God in our lives. While open heavens are all about our relationship with our God, open doors are about our responsibilities to carry out the revealed will of God for our lives in the form of ministries, businesses, and any other duties so His will can be done on earth as it is in heaven. In other words, open doors are opportunities God gives us to manage Kingdom business by fulfilling our prophetic destiny. Paul referred to open doors when he talked about the ministry opportunities the Lord gave him. The Lord told the church of Philadelphia:

> "I know your deeds. See, I have placed before you an open door that no one can shut."
> —Revelation 3:8

Our Lord gave the church of Philadelphia open doors because of their faithfulness with what they were given and their trust in His words. He is the One Who has the Key of David to open and close doors, according to His eternal plans and perfect will. The Lord not only gives us open doors, but He also gives us breakthrough by going through doors before us to open them, to remove and subdue everything under our feet. He removes mountains of opposition by anointing and working with us. The New Testament pattern is working with God. "The Lord worked with them and confirmed his word by the signs that accompanied it" (Mark 16:20). That means God's plan for us is to be fruitful in the work He assigned to each person. At the end of His ministry, Jesus told God the Father that He had completed what the Father gave Him to do and had brought glory to Him. In other words, Jesus stayed under open heavens and walked through every open door the Father placed before Him.

The challenge is to stay under open heavens when the favor of God opens doors, or when challenges and oppositions start raging. The tendency during times of trials or successes is to focus on them, rather than on Him. We are to stay under open heavens and walk through open doors of opportunities. The goal of the enemy is to tempt us to wander away from being under an open heaven. We are often tempted to view the success of a ministry as an end in itself and neglect our relationship with God, family, and covenant people in our lives. If we continue that route, before long we start hiding from our relationship and His voice in our responsibilities, just as Adam did in the Garden of Eden. Very soon, we start using our work or ministry to cover our shortcomings. Others get discouraged because of the opposition. Every man and woman of God who lived for the glory of God by maximizing the opportunity they were given went through these challenges. Even the Lord Jesus told the church in Philadelphia that He had placed an open door before them in the midst of trial and persecution. He was reassuring the church that since He has the master key over all the opposition on earth, nothing can shut or take away the opportunities He gave her.

The Apostle Paul highlighted very similar things in his ministry and calling as an apostle when he said, "Because a great door for effective work has opened to me, and there are many who oppose me" (1 Corinthians 16:9). He further described, in detail, the intensity of the opposition he faced in walking through the open door of ministry, in obedience to the revealed will of God for his life (2 Corinthians 11:23–28). Two powerful things are in opposition when we go through open doors. The first one is that Jesus Himself promised no opposition can shut the door He opens. His calling is irreversible and unstoppable by the option of our enemies. This is what we witnessed throughout the Bible.

The call of Ezra and Nehemiah is classic for that type of opposition. Their enemies used many strategies to stop them from rebuilding the temple and the wall of Jerusalem. Some of the methods they used included offering to join the work, discouraging the people, making the people afraid, hiring counselors to work against them, frustrating the plan for rebuilding, accusing falsely, intimidating legally, using force— and the list continues. Despite the many clever strategies their enemies used to make them miss the open door of rebuilding, they stood firm and finished the task of rebuilding both the temple and the wall of Jerusalem. Because of their determination and faithfulness, the Lord sent two prophets, Haggai and Zechariah, to renew their spirits and rebuild their hope and confidence. Without inner strength, it's impossible to overcome the spirit of discouragement and ongoing opposition. That is what makes true prophetic ministry so valuable. It brings encouragement, inspiration, edification, correction, direction, affirmation, and enlightenment.

This is the reason it is so important to stay under open heavens to hear the voice of God to overcome the enemy in fulfilling the calling. It is so important to remember in using the open door that the war is with evil spiritual forces. These forces use systems and people to hinder the work in God's Kingdom. The good news is that since we have the Word of the Lord, we can overcome the enemy and complete God's work. The weapons we fight with are not the weapons of this world. On the contrary, "they have divine power to demolish strongholds" (2 Corinthians 10:4). Because of this, we are more than conquerors in Jesus Christ, our Lord. We can say just like Jesus, "I have brought you glory on earth by completing the work you gave me to do" (John 17:4).

Another important point to remember during the opposition is that God gives not only power, but also His supernatural wisdom. He gives generously to His children for the asking. He promised His people,

> "I will give you words and wisdom that none of your adversaries will be able to resist or contradict."
> —Luke 21:15

This truth was demonstrated in the Early Church. However, opposition arose. These men began to argue with Stephen, but they could not stand up against his wisdom or the Spirit by whom he spoke (Acts 6:9–10). As a result, the gospel advanced rapidly around the known world. The power of the gospel was demonstrated for salvation and deliverance in spite of all the resistance, since what He opens no one can shut.

Our responsibility is to understand the schemes of the enemy and stand firm by faith. We overcome opposition not by negotiating, but by trusting the One Who has the key. "This is the victory that has overcome the world, even our faith" (1 John 5:4). In any opposition, we must stand on the eternal truth. "Don't be afraid. . . . Those who are with us are more than those who are with them" (2 Kings 6:16). When we do that, we see the salvation and deliverance of the Lord. Our strength is renewed to finish the race with passion, Holy Spirit fire, and strong faith, because what He opens no one can shut.

Questions for Reflection and Discussion

1. What does the notion of "redeeming time" mean to you? How have you experienced that in your life until now? What additional work toward "redeeming time" might be good to pursue, in light of the teaching in this chapter?
2. What stands out from your reading of the parable in Matthew 25:1–13 found in this chapter?
3. What are the keys to staying "under open heavens"?

CHAPTER 12

OPEN DOORS BEFORE YOU

"See, I have placed before you an open door
that no one can shut."
—Revelation 3:8

These words from the Book of Revelation comprise one of the greatest promises the Lord gave to His church, as well as to individual believers. The foundation of this promise is the absolute authority of the Lord Jesus. Since He has the Key of David, no one in all the universe can challenge His authority. He is also the door for us. Every believer is given opportunities to go through Him without any special title or trademark.

OPEN DOOR—A SIGN OF NEW OPPORTUNITIES

When the Lord says that He has placed an open door before us, His people, He shows us new opportunities that we haven't realized. The phrase "before you" is all about what He has prepared for us. It is about our future! The Apostle Paul summarized this eternal truth.

However, as it is written:
"No eye has seen,
no ear has heard,
no mind has conceived
what God has prepared for those who love him."
—1 Corinthians 2:9

The open door He has set before us is in reference to what He has prepared before earth's foundation in Jesus Christ our Lord. That is why the only true door goes through what He has for us. This is a part of a new beginning with Him. The open door that He has placed before us is a door of freedom from past sin and guilt. Going through the open door, Jesus Himself gives us true and lasting freedom from the past. That is why He declared He was anointed and sent to set the captives free and release the oppressed. Jesus's desire is for us to go in and out through Him for all the blessing He has for us. "Anyone who goes through me will be cared for—will freely go in and out and find pasture" (John 10:9, MSG).

Since the door is Jesus Himself, Who goes before us, it has one very important requirement: we must understand the nature of the Kingdom door or gate. God's Kingdom gate, Jesus Christ, is set before His church. It is a narrow gate. Which means there are things we can't take through this gate. The invitation is not to bring anything: "Enter through the narrow gate" (Matthew 7:13). It requires us to live for Christ and trust Him by seeking His will and His Kingdom first. True self-discipline is demanded for facing the challenges that try to hold us back.

The church in Philadelphia received the promise of the open door. The narrow gate has a future great hope and promise when we go through it during challenging and testing times. The Lord saw what they had done by being faithful and true to His name. They didn't have much strength to resist the test. The Lord saw their willingness to go through such a narrow, difficult door. He promised when He placed an open door in front of them, they would not have to depend upon their strength to open it, but just to go through it. After the trial, they discovered the open door and narrow road that leads to life, and the future hope and promises of the Lord.

Willingness to go through the narrow gate takes us into new open doors of opportunities to fulfill our purpose and calling. This forces us to let go of past things that are not relevant for the new assignment for the new season. This is just like boarding our flight for a new destination.

Over the past two decades or more, airline passengers have been asked to remove their shoes as part of the routine security check before boarding. This can be a frustrating process that seems to take too much time, yet it has a vital purpose to check where a passenger's feet have been.

The X-ray can screen for items of concern that might be detected inside shoes. Modern technology also allows security officers to blow a puff of air on the shoes and immediately screen for chemicals. This reveals, to some extent, where the shoes have traveled in the past and can warn of potential danger for fellow passengers.

The Holy Spirit does a similar check to reveal what we should take off in order to walk through the door of destiny. It is crucial that believers take off things they have been carrying from past places—physical, emotional, or spiritual. Their lives have not matched Kingdom values. You simply can't cleanse the harmful traces of where you've been without divine intervention.

This said, other reasons might cause you to take off or let go, for the joy and blessings that would wait for those who are willing to go through the narrow gate to enter the wide field of new opportunities.

Our relationship with God is by grace, because of His wonderful mercy. God's mercy revises the judgment we deserve. Grace provides unjustifiable provision to qualify us to have access to His presence through the true door, Jesus Christ Himself. Grace places us in everlasting relationship with God, the Creator and Redeemer. God's total package of revised judgment is released: undeserved forgiveness and His love signify His favor is being released.

God's favor is what qualifies us to go through the open door to fulfill His purpose on earth as ambassadors of His Kingdom. This is the core of biblical Christianity. We must also consider a cost to the biblical life of discipleship.

The cost of representing God on earth begins with personal holiness. Holiness entails being set apart for God. The fundamental issue in being set apart as an ambassador of God's Kingdom is letting go of things that hold us back.

Abraham was the first leader in the Bible who was told to let go of his country, his people, and his father's household. God's mission was for Abraham to become a father and leader of nations. In obedience to God's calling, Abraham let go of everything and became a friend of God, a father of many nations, and a blessing to all humanity.

The second leader was Moses, who let go of his past to go into the new. Moses knew his call and embraced it with his whole heart. He waited for the right timing to lead God's people to freedom. Moses was willing to pay the full price for his leadership call. The first thing Moses let go of for the sake of his leadership was the pleasure of Egypt (Hebrews 11:24–27). This pleasure includes the privilege he had as a grandson of Pharaoh, the monarch of Egypt. With this, he also rejected the honor that came with social status: his title, his name, his Egyptian power, and authority. For Moses, all these were temporary. They didn't relate to his destiny. Moses not only refused the pleasure of Egypt, but he also "chose to be mistreated along with the people of God rather than to enjoy the pleasures of sin for a short time" (Hebrews 11:25).

After Moses waited 80 years for the Lord, the Lord revealed Himself to him. However, before God would commission Moses for the new open door, He asked the prophet to take off his shoes. God called to him from within the burning bush, "Moses! Moses!" And Moses said, "Here I am." "Do not come any closer," God said. "Take off your sandals, for the place where you are standing is holy ground" (Exodus 3:4–5).

Moses's shoes represented 80 years of life's experiences, including these:

- A sense of failure, because after he killed an Egyptian guard to help his people their situation became worse;
- Fear, as he ran from Pharaoh simply to stay alive rather than improving his people's lot in Egypt;
- Rejection, as the Hebrews in Egypt refused to recognize Moses as one of their own, much less as a leader. As a result, Moses became a shepherd of his father-in-law's sheep in the wilderness, unaware of his future and the future of his people.

This is why the first thing the Lord told Moses, before commissioning him as the leader of his people, was to take off his shoes. Moses had to let go of the past for the sake of his future. That is breaking out from the past in order to break through into the future. Taking off his shoes signified exactly that for Moses. Once those shoes were off, Moses was ready to take the good news of deliverance to the nation of Israel, who had been under a heavy yoke of oppression for more than 400 years. By asking Moses to take off his shoes, the Lord was saying to Moses, "Let go of any part of your past that might hinder your effectiveness in the new assignment."

Taking off one's shoes also speaks about holy reverence with worship, awe, respect, and fear for God. This was certainly the case with Moses, who took off his shoes and covered his face in holy reverence to the manifested presence of God—making the dried-up wilderness of Horeb holy ground.

Now, as then, taking off one's old shoes also allows the right kind of shoes to take their place with authority as well as readiness. "Having strapped on YOUR FEET THE GOSPEL OF PEACE IN PREPARATION [to face the enemy with firm-footed stability and the readiness produced by the good news]" (Ephesians 6:15, AMP).

The angel of the Lord asked Joshua a similar thing. After Moses's death, Joshua took leadership and prepared the people to enter and possess the land of their inheritance. After they crossed the Jordan River, before they destroyed the city of Jericho the commander of the army of the Lord stood before Joshua. Joshua asked the angel, "Are you for us or for our enemies?" (Joshua 5:13). His answer was "neither." When Joshua asked him what message he had, the commander of the Lord's army replied, "'Take off your sandals, for the place where you are standing is holy.' And Joshua did so" (Joshua 5:15). In this case again, Joshua's removal of his shoes was about reverence, submission, and letting go of 40 years of wilderness experience. To face Jericho and all the enemies they fought after Jericho and in order to possess the land, Joshua had to remove his old shoes. That way, he could walk in authority for victory through the open door.

In this sense, it is crucial that every believer who would like to go through the narrow gate take off things that might hinder running God's race and accomplishing God's purpose. For example, after Saul placed his armor on David, David took off Saul's armor before he went out to kill Goliath, the enemy of God's people.

Taking off old shoes is also a sign of coming freedom. After the Lord raised Lazarus from death, He told those in attendance to take off Lazarus's grave clothes, which reflected the place that, a few moments before, had held Lazarus captive. "The dead man came out, his hands and feet wrapped with strips of linen, and a cloth around his face. Jesus said to them, 'Take off the grave clothes and let him go'" (John 11:44). Jesus commanded that they take off what was a sign of death. Then, as now, a culture of unbelief could bury what was intended for the glory of God. Taking off your shoes shows the beautiful feet that will provide the footprints a generation can see clearly and follow. The Word of God talks about our walk with Jesus and for Jesus far more than about our face or our activities. A believer's feet tell the story of walking through life or life's experiences. The authority of a child of God comes far more from walking with Him than doing things for Him. The Lord showed the importance of this when He said to Abraham, His friend, "I am God Almighty; walk before me and be blameless" (Genesis 17:1).

In the case of the disciples, Jesus washed their feet to give them feet that were beautiful enough to qualify them for the New Testament ministry. In their case, as is the case of anyone who would be the Lord's messenger, the question is, "How beautiful, suitable, and fitting are your feet to go through the narrow door God has put before you?"

OPEN DOOR—A SIGN OF SPECIAL GIFT

Open doors are a very special gift from the Lord both to be fruitful and to accomplish His will on earth. In our culture, there is a saying that "Time is money." This is to show the importance of time or its worth or value. However, in my opinion, time is more than money, since we can't buy time with monetary value. Time is life! The special gift of God to every child of God is time. That is the opportunity that we ought to maximize to advance His Kingdom and to serve His purpose. That is why He said to the church at Philadelphia, "See, I have placed before you an open door that no one can shut" (Revelation 3:8). This is His special gift that no one can take away from the faithful church. It is given for multiplication and fruitfulness.

- **Passing through the narrow places**
Training in the ministry shows us how to keep going beyond the obstacles and hindrances that stop us from walking through the open door to be fruitful in the Kingdom of God. Determination is the key to redeeming the time. The Lord uses the trial the enemy brings to stop us from moving forward to change us into His image and building our character to fulfill our calling. This has been the case for everyone who has lived for the glory of God and used their time wisely to honor him. Joseph's life was just one example. "Joseph, sold as a slave. They bruised his feet with shackles, his neck was put in irons, till what he foretold came to pass, till the word of the LORD proved him true" (Psalm 105:17–19). That hardship didn't stop him but qualified him to become the ruler of Egypt and to save lives in many nations. We see a similar situation in the Apostle Paul's life (2 Corinthians 11).

- **Removing limitation—break out by taking off the veil over us**
One of the challenging things is to create a fence around our past successes or setbacks. But the idea of the open door is willingness to remove those limitations or fences in order to advance by going through the open door. We can only maximize the gift God has trusted us with if we have courage to move forward in spite of opposition. Doors are to walk through, so we can go beyond all the limitations. Paul referred to a similar situation when he said, "Because a great door for effective work has opened to me, and there are many who oppose me" (1 Corinthians 16:9). We go through open doors by removing limitations by faith and refusing opposition through courage and trust in the Lord.

- **Plowing the ground**
The gift of the new season is to prepare the ground for a new harvest by overcoming discouragement and working hard. Breaking new ground is hard work. It is preparing the soil

for the future seed by faith without knowing what the next season will look like. It will be possible only if a person hears and obeys His voice, is at the right place, walks in the fear of the Lord, sees open doors (opportunities God gives us) and believes Jesus came to open the heavens, so that we can walk through open doors.

- **Understanding the time or the season of harvest**
  Open doors are for gathering in the harvest. The Lord Jesus challenged His disciples for a lack of understanding about the season of harvest. "Don't you say, 'It's still four months until harvest'? I tell you, open your eyes and look at the fields! They are ripe for harvest" (John 4:35). Jesus chose to do the will of His Father instead of having dinner with them, because He understood the season of harvest. The season of harvest is a sign of open doors. That is when what was waiting to start became real. It is a season of hearing, understanding, and responding to the call of reaching out to those who are ready to respond to the gospel. It is a season of new hope and change. It is seeing again, hearing again, dreaming again, hoping again, rejoicing again.

> See! The winter is past;
>   the rains are over and gone.
> Flowers appear on the earth;
>   the season of singing has come,
>   the cooing of doves
>   is heard in our land.
> —Song of Solomon 2:11–12

The Apostle Paul took this concept to the next level and connected it with the harvest, a time of salvation. He showed us that there is a special grace God releases for the time of the harvest. He encouraged the believers in Corinth not to waste the grace that is given for gathering harvest:

As God's co-workers we urge you not to receive God's grace in vain. For he says,

"In the time of my favor I heard you,
and in the day of salvation I helped you."

I tell you, now is the time of God's favor, now is the day of salvation.
—2 Corinthians 6:1–2

What a powerful verse about the grace of harvest and the need to understand the now time.

The primary reason for open doors is for the salvation of the lost, which was the focus of Jesus Christ during His earthly ministry. He Himself said, "For the Son of Man came to seek and to save the lost" (Luke 19:10). His final command was for His disciples to go into all the world and preach the gospel and make disciples in the nations. His promise was that as long as they did that, He would protect them and draw people to Himself and confirm His Word with signs and wonders.

The reason many Christians around the world admired Dr. Billy Graham was that he became an example to all the Christians who are committed to proclaim the gospel of salvation faithfully. Graham's unwavering faithfulness to the gospel inspires and strengthens me as I look back on nearly 50 years of a similar calling on my own life. I accepted the call to preach the gospel when I was in the ninth grade. I was attending a summer Bible school in Ethiopia, taught by missionaries. One of my teachers was Peter Cottrell, a missionary from London, who was teaching the Epistle of Romans. One day, without explanation, Cottrell began the class by reading Daniel 12:3.

Those who are wise will shine like the brightness of the heavens, and those who lead many to righteousness, like the stars for ever and ever.

As I mentioned in the introduction, the call of God that I accepted 53 years ago still burns in my heart. That is why I am committed to continue preaching the gospel, training and equipping emerging leaders, and encouraging and empowering the Body of Christ to fulfill the mandate of the gospel. Preaching the gospel is the New Testament believers' mandate. Not everyone is an evangelist, but everyone is given the mandate of presenting the gospel by using every open door. He is the One Who gives us open doors and protects us as He did for Paul: "Now when I went to Troas to preach the gospel of Christ and found that the Lord had opened a door for me" (2 Corinthians 2:12). The Lord said to Paul, "Do not be afraid; keep on speaking, do not be silent. For I am with you, and no one is going to attack and harm you, because I have many people in this city" (Acts 18:9–10). This is the time for the Body of Christ, worldwide, to use every open door to declare the gospel of the Kingdom and salvation.

Questions for Reflection and Discussion

1. Reflect on your "new beginning with Christ" (however recent or distant that beginning took place). What do you remember about it? What were the steps to the new beginning? What hope did it bring into your life?

2. What might we need to "take off" in order to go through the narrow gate?

3. If "preaching the gospel is the New Testament believers' mandate," how can you respond to that call? What are the gifts you bring in response to the grace and mercy of God in your life?

PART THREE

WHEN HE
Opens
FOR
CROSSING OVER

CHAPTER 13

WHEN HE OPENS TO CROSS OVER

C rossing over is about movement that implies a change of position, location, attitude, value, thinking, and paradigm. It is an indication of going from one side to the other. One Merriam-Webster Dictionary definition of crossover is "an instance of breaking into another category."

Such movement or driving is what God placed in us as a part of our nature as human beings. This gives every healthy, normal person a desire for progress, improvement, advancement, evolution, and personal social development. It is human distinctiveness or characteristic to strive for a change.

Hence, crossing over overcomes some of the stoppages in order to reach the desired destination. In this case, crossing over is part of the human development and progress for greater achievement. It's a process of overcoming hindrances and limitations to reach the desired goal. Such God-given, natural longing for change and transformation enhances creativity, persistence, and resolve to move on to go to the other side. Such a natural process is called crossing over or overpassing a viaduct. Actions of crossing over include determination and commitment. Just like a hurdle race, which demands jumping or leaping over barriers to win the race, it also requires focus, faith, and more.

GOD'S INVITATION

An invitation for crossing over was initiated by God for us to have a relationship with Him through salvation. Therefore, a true invitation for crossing over starts with our salvation through the work of Christ on the cross. Thus, the cross of Christ is the true bridge for crossing over between death and life. From the time the first Adam was separated from God by death, God's invitation has been to bring us back to Himself by asking us where we are, so that we can cross over again to go to where He is. All through the Bible, God's call has been to repent from our sins and to come to Him for forgiveness of all our sins.

> "Come now, let us settle the matter,"
>   says the LORD.
>   "Though your sins are like scarlet,
>   they shall be as white as snow;
>   though they are red as crimson,
>   they shall be like wool."
> —Isaiah 1:18–19

God the Father extended that invitation to us by sending His only begotten Son, the Lord Jesus Christ, Who came to seek and save the lost. During His earthly ministry, the Lord Jesus illustrated the urgency to cross over before it is too late to do so, by using the parable of the rich man and Lazarus, a vivid picture of the reality of life and death.

There once was a rich man, expensively dressed in the latest fashions, wasting his days in conspicuous consumption. A poor man named Lazarus, covered with sores, had been dumped on his doorstep. All he lived for was to get a meal from scraps off the rich man's table. His best friends were the dogs who came and licked his sores.

Then he died, this poor man, and was taken up by the angels to the lap of Abraham. The rich man also died and was buried. In hell and in torment, he looked up and saw Abraham in the distance and Lazarus in his lap. He called out, "Father Abraham, mercy! Have mercy! Send Lazarus to dip his finger in water to cool my tongue. I'm in agony in this fire."

But Abraham said, "Child, remember that in your lifetime you got the good things and Lazarus the bad things. It's not like that here. Here he's consoled and you're tormented. Besides, in all these matters there is a huge chasm set between us so that no one can go from us to you, even if he wanted to, nor can anyone cross over from you to us."

—Luke 16:19–26, MSG

In this parable a number of things are shown about crossing over before it is too late to do so. The rich man didn't pay attention to eternity or life after physical death. By nature, everyone is spiritually dead because of sin. "As for you, you were dead in your transgressions and sins" (Ephesians 2:1). The rich man didn't realize this truth until it was too late. The only way to cross over is through the cross of Christ. By accepting Him as the only way, truth, and life, a person crosses over from death to life: "God . . . made us alive with Christ even when we were dead in transgressions—it is by grace you have been saved" (Ephesians 2:4–5). As we read in the above story, there is a great chasm that is impossible to cross over, because it is a gap between life and death. A person can cross this abyss by accepting Christ Jesus as their personal Savior.

Therefore, true salvation is crossing over from death to life through the cross of Christ. The Lord Jesus puts it this way: "Very truly I tell you, whoever hears my word and believes him who sent me has eternal life and will not be judged but *has crossed over from death to life*" (John 5:24, emphasis added).

Hence, God's eternal invitation is to come to Him in order to cross over from death to life by accepting the invitation of salvation. When a person invites Christ Jesus into their life, he or she becomes a new creation by crossing over from death to life through the power of the Resurrection, since Jesus Christ is the life and the resurrection. For those who have crossed over through Christ Jesus, there will not be any condemnation or eternal judgment of sin that we read about in the above parable. When we cross over, we receive new life and the forgiveness of our sin. That means we are not the enemies of God anymore. Rather, we become children of God. "Yet to all who did receive him, to those who believed in his name, he gave the right to become children of God" (John 1:12).

In this context, crossing over is becoming sons and daughters of the living God by receiving eternal life and the spirit of adoption that makes us partakers of the divine nature. That gives us the right to call God "Abba, Father." That is the true crossing over from death to life. In accepting the invitation, a person crosses over from being the enemy of God to becoming a child of God. Such crossing over changes us from being sinners to saints of the Most High and moves us from the kingdom of darkness to the Kingdom of light. "Giving joyful thanks to the Father, who has qualified you to share in the inheritance of his holy people in the kingdom of light" (Colossians 1:12). Through the crossing over, He gives us His righteousness. "God made him who had no sin to be sin for us, so that in him we might become the righteousness of God" (2 Corinthians 5:21). This qualifies us not only to become a new creation, but also to be an ambassador of the Kingdom of light with all spiritual authority for His glory.

Furthermore, such a call of God enables us to cross over to be changed into the likeness of Jesus Christ by justification through faith and daily sanctification and holiness to reflect His glory. "And those he predestined, he also called; those he called, he also justified; those he justified, he also glorified" (Romans 8:30).

In the process of crossing over, the second phase of our salvation is overcoming the acts of the flesh (Galatians 5:19–21), since those who practice them will face the judgment of God. "I warn you, as I did before, that those who live like this will not inherit the kingdom of God" (Galatians 5:21). When we crossed over, we received the power of the Holy Spirit to overcome the work of the flesh and walk in the Spirit.

Those who belong to Christ Jesus have crucified the sinful nature with its passions and desires. Since we live by the Spirit, let us keep in step with the Spirit.
—Galatians 5:24–25

Doing this enables us to bear the fruits of the spirit for the glory of God:

But the fruit of the Spirit is love, joy, peace, forbearance, kindness, goodness, faithfulness, gentleness and self-control.
—Galatians 5:22–23.

Crossing over, according to divine invitation, is from the old to the new with our own free will, since whoever is in Christ is a new creation. Therefore, the critical issue is not arguing whether a believer can sin or not, but the concern should be whether a person has crossed over. When we cross over, we take off our old nature and put on a new nature that reflects internal transformation.

This is why the New Testament invitation is about relationship for an internal change more than external appearance. Throughout the New Testament, the Lord's invitation is "follow me."

> Whoever serves me must follow me; and where I am, my servant also will be. My Father will honor the one who serves me.
> —John 12:26

Therefore, the invitation to cross over is not only to be saved before it is too late, but also to be with the Lord. That means moving from condemnation, fear, guilt, hopelessness, and darkness to an extraordinary relationship with the Lord of light, life, and peace. It's entering into the fullness of His presence through the door the Lord Himself has opened for whoever will. Hence, the core of this invitation is to go through Him, our true door, for eternal joy and everlasting life. This invitation is for whoever will!

We will turn now to a deeper look at God's invitation to cross over.

Questions for Reflection and Discussion

1. In what ways have you sensed the crossover "movement or driving" of what God has placed in our nature as human beings?

2. What stands out most vividly for you in the parable found in Luke 16:19–26 as found in this chapter? What about that story prompts it to stand out?

3. If you received God's invitation to "cross over" for salvation, ponder the story of how that came about. What were the steps? Who played important parts in that story? If you have not received that invitation, how might you respond now?

CHAPTER 14

GOD'S INVITATION TO CROSS OVER

Crossing over is the desire of God for His people. It is a part of His covenant plan. God has a plan for every individual, as well as for every family and every nation who submits to His eternal plan. This is the reason He declared over the covenant people, when they were in captivity without any foreseeable future and hope, by saying, "'For I know the plans that I have for you,' declares the LORD, 'plans to prosper you and not to harm you, plans to give you hope and a future'" (Jeremiah 29:11). Crossing over is the only way to enter into God's covenantal blessings that are prepared for us because of His eternal and unchanging love. He showed us this through the life and journey of the nation of Israel.

God's invitation to cross over is for true and lasting freedom. After our salvation, God's invitation is to move us through an open door to the other side for a life of victory. In the Old Testament, this reality was illustrated by the Israelites' journey from Egypt to the Promised Land. They started the journey of crossing over through the Passover, a sign of protection by the blood. That was a prophetic picture of our salvation from slavery to Satan and the misery of sin and death. By crossing over, the Jewish people overcame the 430 years of suffering to start a journey of freedom. God remembered the covenant He had made with His friend Abraham and came down to help with their crossing over to the land of promise and inheritance. When He heard their cry and suffering under the heavy yoke of slavery, He came down because of His eternal plan to help them cross over. "So I have come down to deliver them from the power of the Egyptians and to bring them up out of that land into a good and spacious land, a land flowing with milk and honey" (Exodus 3:8). The phrase "I have come down to deliver them" is very important in order to understand the process and purpose of crossing over, as we will see through the pages of this book.

THE COMMAND TO GET READY

Crossing over was not a matter of opinion or convenience, but the command of the Lord to go through what He had opened. The Lord wanted them to get ready, get up, arise, prepare, proceed, and surge to cross over or transit because of the time. In this, He was telling them that the journey of 40 years was over, and the time of moving forward was now, and it required special preparation. The Lord was not asking them just to move forward the way they had in the past, but with an understanding of a new season and a letting go of past experience on the journey through the wilderness. They would be going around the same mountain without purpose and focus on entering into the promises of His blessings. The new journey of crossing over requires an unshakable mindset and a change of attitude. In the journey of crossing over, a paradigm shift is a major part of preparation, since a change of value system is required for what is coming. In order to get ready to cross over, it is important to know the change of season.

In the case of Joshua, the Lord made it so clear about the change of season: "Moses my servant is dead" (Joshua 1:2). That means the old order was over. The generation who had refused to cross over into the Promised Land 40 years before was now gone. That was the generation Moses had brought out of Egypt that was controlled by fear and unbelief. Now it was Joshua's turn to lead the new generation into the Promised Land. This was a generation that had emerged for the new season. Until that time, Joshua himself was part of Moses's generation, but Caleb and Joshua separated themselves from the generation that refused to cross over (Numbers 13 and 14). The faith they had in their God gave them a different spirit to obey God wholeheartedly. Hence, the Lord gave Joshua a second chance after 40 years of waiting. The death of Moses was a sign of the end of the past season; it was an open door for the new leadership to cross over.

Then the question is, what does preparation or getting ready require?

THE COMMAND TO CROSS OVER

"After the death of Moses, the servant of the Lord, the Lord said to Joshua son of Nun, Moses' aide: 'Moses my servant is dead. Now then, you and all these people, get ready to cross the Jordan River into the land I am about to give to them—to the Israelites. I will give you every place where you set your foot, as I promised Moses'" (Joshua 1:1–3).

This was a command for Joshua to talk the people into the promise by passing over and crossing over the Jordan River. It was coming out of the wilderness. The first crossing over was the Red Sea under the leadership of Moses, when they came out of Egypt. The Lord revealed Himself to Moses to send him back to Egypt to tell the people about God's invitation for crossing over to freedom with divine guidance, protection, and provision. With a greater divine intervention, finally, they came out victoriously to freedom with favor and provision. That was a true crossing over for lasting freedom and according to God's promises. Hence, God's command was to cross over to experience the blessings of the covenant of Abraham as they entered into a lasting relationship through true worship after they had crossed over the Red Sea. The Red Sea was the sign of true crossing over from slavery to freedom as they watched the deliverance of the Lord once and for all. That was the reason Moses told the people, "Do not be afraid. Stand firm and you will see the deliverance the LORD will bring you today. The Egyptians you see today you will never see again. The LORD will fight for you; you need only to be still" (Exodus 14:13–14). That was the true crossing over to the other side, since they would never see their enemies again, and they were not able to go back. Lasting victory over their enemies forever was signified by the final crossing over through the open door. The door was the door of miracles.

Such a crossing over for salvation produces the joy of salvation, which results in true praises and worship of God.

The test of freedom is our ability to worship God with sincere faith, a pure heart, and a clear conscience. That was why Moses wrote a worship song for the Israelites to start praising the Lord for opening the Red Sea for them to cross over into a place of freedom to worship. Miriam stepped up to lead the worship.

Then Miriam the prophetess, Aaron's sister, took a tambourine in her hand, and all the women followed her, with tambourines and dancing. Miriam sang to them:

Sing to the LORD,
for he is highly exalted.
The horse and driver
he has hurled into the sea.
—Exodus 15:20–21

That was the first crossing over for them. Every true crossing over brings results in the praises of the God of miracles. However, at every true crossing over, we need to overcome challenges. Crossing over is warring for our freedom. For the Israelites, crossing meant escaping the grip of their enemy for the foreseeable future and moving into their inheritance. They were passing through the narrow gate God had opened for them to go to the other side. Therefore, among other things, crossing over is a place of separation from the past to move into our promised future. That is a sign of triumph for those who are crossing over, while it is a permanent defeat for the enemy. That is the reason war gets intensified at the crossing over, particularly as it relates to our salvation.

This is the time the Lord is commanding them to cross over again to enter the Promised Land. The wilderness was where they were for a long time, and it was a place they were accustomed to. It was the place where they saw many of God's signs and wonders. It was a place of life, a miracle after more than 40 years. They experienced God's guidance day and night (cloud and pillar of fire), provision (food, angels, and water from a rock), protection from their enemies, and more. Now, the Lord was ready to take them through transition to help them cross over into their blessings. The promise is a blessing, both in creation and through covenant. After He created them in His image, male and female, He blessed them. That was God's plan from the beginning. When He called Abraham, He made a covenant to bless him and to make him a blessing to the nations.

Therefore, God's desire is to bless His people. Miracles are His compassionate intervention to shorten the process or to solve problems to help His people cross over into their blessings. Hence, a miracle is a bridge the Lord provides to help us move on into our blessings. Miracles deal with problems or issues of life that would hinder us from reaching our potential, a life of blessings in Christ Jesus. They deal with temporal things so that we can focus on eternal things. We need miracles for what we see and face that is beyond our ability and resources. That is why the Word encourages us to focus on what is eternal.

> So we fix our eyes not on what is seen, but on what is unseen. For what is seen is temporary, but what is unseen is eternal.
> —2 Corinthians 4:18

The Israelites, who had become accustomed to the miracles of God for 40 years in the wilderness, had lost their appetite for the greater blessings they were created and delivered for when they left the slavery of Egypt. Now, the Lord was challenging them to cross over into the blessing, the original plan and purpose for which they had started the journey. They had to be willing to come out of the wilderness and a life of miracles in order to cross over into the land of blessings. That was the command to "cross over."

THE PROMISE OF CROSSING OVER: "I WILL GIVE YOU."

"I will give you every place where you set your foot" (Joshua 1:3). The starting place is to get ready. The destination is moving toward possessing the Promised Land, our blessings. It is full entry into the will and purpose of God to please Him and enjoy His presence. The process is crossing over the Jordan by coming out of the wilderness. In order to come out and move forward to cross over, Joshua and the Israelites were encouraged to pay attention to the following:

First, accepting fully the new leader for the new season. When the Lord said, "Moses my servant is dead," He was not telling the bad news of the death of Moses but affirming the change of season they had to embrace in order to move forward. Emotional attachment to the past has a very strong hold. Among other things, it causes a person to miss God's timing. The story of Samuel, Saul, and David is one of the best examples for such challenges. God told Samuel to anoint Saul as king over Israel because of their desire to have a king like other nations did. After Samuel anointed Saul, the spirit of God came upon Saul to lead the people of God. He started with great humility, but before long, he disobeyed God and would not wait for the Lord's timing.

When Saul felt that Samuel was late and the people were scattering out of fear, he decided to make a fellowship offering to keep the people from going to war. "He said, 'Bring me the burnt offering and the fellowship offerings.' And Saul offered up the burnt offering" (1 Samuel 13:9). However, he didn't save any time by disobeying the Lord. "Just as he finished making the offering, Samuel arrived, and Saul went out to greet him" (v. 10). Samuel was very disappointed. His question was, "What have you done?" (v. 11). After King Saul explained his action, Samuel gave him this message, "But now your kingdom will not endure; the Lord has sought out a man after his own heart and appointed him leader of his people, because you have not kept the Lord's command" (v. 14).

Despite Saul's disobedience, the Lord gave him another chance to go and destroy the enemy of the people of God, the Amalekites. But he failed again by pleasing the people, instead of destroying everything: "But Saul and the army spared Agag and the best of the sheep and cattle, the fat calves and lambs—everything that was good" (1 Samuel 15:9). That grieved the Lord. Samuel told the final message of the Lord to King Saul, "Because you have rejected the word of the Lord, he has rejected you as king" (1 Samuel 15:23). That day Saul's kingdom was given to David.

However, even after such a clear message from the Lord, the Prophet Samuel had a hard time letting go of King Saul. He also didn't ask the Lord who he should anoint in the place of Saul. But he kept weeping for Saul, the one the Lord rejected. Unfortunately, he didn't see David, the one the Lord had already anointed and prepared for the new season. Emotional attachment is one of the difficult things to let go of during the transition to crossing over. For the Lord had come and said, "How long will you mourn for Saul, since I have rejected him as king over Israel? Fill your horn with oil and be on your way; I am sending you to Jesse of Bethlehem. I have chosen one of his sons to be king" (1 Samuel 16:1). The Lord didn't challenge him because of emotion. It was with care and prayer, and because of the timing. God was asking, "How long?" After that Samuel accepted David by faith and went to Bethlehem to anoint him. He put the transition into motion for the acceleration of God's purpose. David brought back the Ark of the presence of God that had been neglected during the reign of Saul. The glory was restored, and the promises were secured.

Second, trusting in the protection and guidance of God. The Israelites crossed the Red Sea, but they didn't trust the Lord to lead them to cross over into the Promised Land. This was the command from the Lord, to get up and cross over the Jordan River. It came as a second chance after 40 years. At this time the Lord gave Joshua the assurance of His protection and presence. "No one will be able to stand up against you all the days of your life. As I was with Moses, so I will be with you; I will never leave you nor forsake you" (Joshua 1:5). In the process of crossing, it is very important to overcome fear, doubt, and discouragement by trusting in the Lord and standing on His promises, just as He instructed Joshua: "Be strong and courageous. Do not be afraid; do not be discouraged, for the LORD your God will be with you wherever you go" (Joshua 1:9).

Third, getting ready to cross over. After Joshua accepted the responsibility of leading the people into the Promised Land, they took the following steps:

1. First, they camped by the Jordan River for three days with the anticipation of what the Lord would do. The three days were given to them to consecrate themselves, for the great thing the Lord would do to lead them into the Promised Land by crossing over. After he went through the camp as their new leader, Joshua instructed, "Consecrate yourselves, for tomorrow the LORD will do amazing things among you" (Joshua 3:5). Forty years earlier, Moses had told them a similar thing at Mount Sinai in preparation for the manifestation of the glory of God. "And the LORD said to Moses, 'Go to the people and consecrate them today and tomorrow. Have them wash their clothes and be ready by the third day, because on that day the LORD will come down on Mount Sinai in the sight of all the people'" (Exodus 19:10–11). Yes, the Lord came down that mountain after the preparation on the third day. The mountain was covered with a cloud and smoke, and the whole mountain trembled violently, and the people heard a very loud trumpet blast in their camps that grew louder and louder.

   At that stage, Moses decided to take the people out from their camp to meet with God. Can you image coming closer to that mountain to be in the holy presence of God, with the trumpet blasting and the thick cloud covering the mountain, and the Lord speaking from the fire? No wonder the people asked Moses to speak to them, and not God: "Speak to us yourself and we will listen. But do not have God speak to us or we will die" (Exodus 20:19). The holy reverence of God came upon them when they saw the glory cloud that covered the mountain and heard the voice of God from the fire. In summarizing their experience, Moses said to them, "For what mortal has ever heard the voice of the living God speaking out of fire, as we have, and survived?" (Deuteronomy 5:26). Of course, the answer is, "No other nation!"

I am sure when Joshua went throughout the camp after three days and told the people to be consecrated for the third day, he remembered what took place that day and his own personal experience on Mount Sinai in the presence of God. God also gave him the assurance of His presence: "As I was with Moses, so I will be with you" (Joshua 1:5). Joshua believed that God, Who came down Mount Sinai and shook it 40 years before, would come again to divide the Jordan River if they would take the time to consecrate themselves. On our life journey to cross over, the reason the Lord asks us to wait is so that we can consecrate or purify ourselves by faith in anticipation of great and mighty things He will do for us. Therefore, waiting is not a waste of time, but it is preparation for a great thing God will do for us. That is one of the requirements for crossing over.

They followed Joshua's instructions. One of the reasons they were in the wilderness for so long was that they had refused to obey the leader the Lord had given them, namely Moses. They had made a great effort to appoint a leader of their choosing to lead them back to Egypt. However, this was a new generation, and this was a new season. Joshua instructed them to set themselves apart to be holy by faith for the Lord's visitation for the great thing the Lord would do for them.

2. Second, to follow the Ark of the Lord to cross over, they were to watch for the priests who carried the Ark and follow them, since they had never been this way before. This was a new path that would take them over into their Promised Land. In other words, they had to stop depending on the last

40 years' journey experience. During the 40 years' journey in the wilderness, they were under the pillar of fire and cloud. It was a journey of miracles, guidance, provision, and protection. But since this was a new journey, the Lord wanted them to participate by consecrating themselves, accepting a new path, obeying the Lord, and following the presence of God. The season came for them to move from the life of miracles into the life of His presence and lasting blessings. His presence is the key to crossing over. The Ark was a sign of the presence, power, and covenant of God.

Following the Ark had two dimensions. The first was total submission to the will and way of God. The second was to learn again about God's holy reverence. Keeping a distance between them and the Ark of God was a sign of the fear of the Lord. This was the very sin Ezekiel later challenged the people about by delivering the message of the Lord, "When they placed their threshold next to my threshold and their doorposts beside my doorposts, with only a wall between me and them, they defiled my holy name by their detestable practices" (Ezekiel 43:8). This meant there was no respect for the holiness of God. That made them pay a very heavy price for 70 years in captivity. God extends His mercy and grace to us, but He doesn't compromise on His holiness, since by nature His holiness is like a consuming fire.

3. Third, they obeyed spiritual authority to cross over. The Lord gave Joshua specific instructions about how to take the people into the Promised Land. Joshua told them what to do in order to cross over. The new generation obeyed the voice of their leader and submitted to his authority. In fact, not only did they submit to Joshua's authority to cross over, but also they made a declaration by saying, "Whoever rebels against your word and does not obey it, whatever you may command them, will be put to death. Only be strong and

courageous!" (Joshua 1:18). Such a strong stand enabled them to cross over by following the strategy the Lord gave them through Joshua. Therefore, one of the key elements in crossing over into our Promised Land is following divine orders by submitting to leadership authority.

Sometimes, we face challenges in our pursuit to cross over. In the next chapter, we'll consider how we overcome those challenges and embrace God's promises.

Questions for Reflection and Discussion

1. In the opening section of this chapter the author says, "God's invitation to cross over is for true and lasting freedom." In what ways have you experienced that freedom?

2. The Jeremiah 19:11 passage, noted near the start of this chapter, is a well-known and well-loved Scripture. How do you respond to that passage? What encouragement does it bring to you?

3. How can we "fix our eyes not on what is seen, but on what is unseen" (2 Corinthians 4:18)? How have you been able to do that? What was its impact?

CHAPTER 15

OVERCOMING THE CHALLENGES OF CROSSING OVER

When the Israelites saw that their enemies were pursuing them, they became overwhelmed with fear and doubt. They believed they would be overtaken by their enemies, since they did not have a powerful army to fight the Egyptians and couldn't move forward because of the Red Sea. They thought they were trapped without a way out. The only way they could overcome was by trusting the Lord Who had brought them out with His powerful arm. This is a truth for every crossing over. At the crossing over, the Lord builds our faith by removing all other options that we usually turn to or trust in.

However, the Lord had prepared in advance both protection and an open door to cross over. For protection the angel of the Lord, who was leading them, came between them and their enemies to guard them from behind:

Then the angel of God, who had been traveling in front of Israel's army, withdrew and went behind them. The pillar of cloud also moved from in front and stood behind them, coming between the armies of Egypt and Israel. Throughout the night the cloud brought darkness to the one side and light to the other side; so neither went near the other all night long.

—Exodus 14:19–20

What a beautiful time! When the enemy said that it was over, the Lord responded by releasing His special army for protection and light. The perception of the Lord brought not only security and safety, but also light in darkness. Where the presence of God is, there is light. The light is our security. The same light brought darkness over the enemy's camp. While the people of God enjoyed the light of His glorious presence, the enemy was overwhelmed with the darkness of His anger.

At the same time, Moses was commanded to use his authority to stretch out his hand over the Red Sea. "Then Moses stretched out his hand over the sea, and all that night the LORD drove the sea back with a strong east wind and turned it into dry land. The waters were divided" (Exodus 14:21). Yes, they crossed over on dry land and never saw their enemies again. That is called lasting victory.

However, an intense war isn't only at the Red Sea, but in every crossing over that requires total obedience to the revealed will of God for His children. That was true even during the ministry of Jesus. The story in Matthew 14:22–33 is a very good example. The Lord Jesus told His disciples to cross over to the other side of the lake after He had fed more than 5,000 people with five loaves and two fish. He went to the mountain to pray. With wholehearted obedience, they started their journey with great confidence because of their knowledge of the lake and the miracle they had just witnessed.

Yet, on the journey of crossing over that night, they faced a very serious challenge that tested their faith. After they had gone a long distance, they were tossed around by strong waves. Since they were far into the lake, they couldn't go back to the land. But the wind came against them, and they couldn't move forward either. They were tested until the Lord Jesus came walking on the same waves that they feared. It was toward the morning, sometime between 3 a.m. and 6 a.m. What a challenge of faith! There was nothing to see since it was night. The One Who had told them to cross over was nowhere to be found. He was on the mountain while they were battered by strong waves on the lake, trying their best to cross over and reach the shore.

In the middle of their struggle, the One Who had told them to cross over to the other side came walking on the same waves that were pounding against the boat and trying to stop them. When they saw Him coming walking on the waves, they were terrified. They didn't believe it would be possible for a person to walk on water, much less on such strong waves. They thought that they were seeing some kind of frightening spirit that might kill them. Such is the picture of some of the challenges of crossing over. It is not only the opposition and the resistance that are trying to stop us from going to the other side, but also the fear and unbelief that they create, leading to hopelessness and discouragement. This event is similar to the story of crossing over the Red Sea.

TAKE COURAGE

During such a terrifying experience, the Lord Who had told them to cross over was drawing near—He was walking on their problem. What a picture for one who must trust and obey the word of the Lord to cross over to the other side. While they were crying out in fear, they heard the voice of the Good Shepherd, the protector, provider, and guide, "Take courage, it is I! Do not be afraid!" (Matthew 14:27, AMP). This shows us that first, the Lord Who told us to cross over always watches over us, even in the middle of strong storms. Second, what seems to be impossible for us to overcome in crossing over is under the feet of the Lord Jesus Christ. When we respond to His voice by faith, He makes the challenges of life subject to us. "You made him to have dominion over the works of Your hands; you have put all things under his feet" (Psalm 8:6, AMP). He showed them this truth the way He responded to Peter's question. When Peter heard the Lord's voice, he said, "Lord, if it's you, tell me to come to you on the water." Jesus said, "Come" (Matthew 14:28–29). Peter came out of the boat and started to walk on the stormy waters that the disciples thought would destroy them. Suddenly, the storm was under Peter's feet. Even if only for a few minutes, Peter walked on the same waves that had tried all night to keep the disciples from crossing over. Yes, when we are with Jesus Christ, there is no power that will stop us from crossing over. After the Lord Jesus boarded their boat, He spoke to the storm; it calmed down, and they crossed over immediately.

Not only do the storms of life resist us or try to stop us from crossing over in the absence of the Lord, but they also do this even when the Lord is with us in our boat. In other words, the challenges we face are not indications of sin or a broken relationship with the Lord. The Lord didn't promise us the absence of storms; instead, He promised us victory in the midst of challenges.

When you pass through the waters,
I will be with you;
and when you pass through the rivers,
they will not sweep over you.
When you walk through the fire,
you will not be burned;
the flames will not set you ablaze.
—Isaiah 43:2

What an amazing promise! The Lord Jesus illustrated this again on another occasion when He said to the disciples, "Let us go over to the other side" (Mark 4:35). However, just as in the other instance, a huge storm came up to stop them from crossing over to the other side, even though He was with them in the boat. When the disciples felt that their boat was threatening to sink at any minute, they cried out in great fear and panic. They woke the Lord Jesus and said to him, "Teacher, don't you care if we drown?" (Mark 4:38). What a separation! When they awakened Him, He started foundational steps needed to master the crossing over to the other side in the midst of challenges:

First, appropriate the use of Jesus's God-given authority. Jesus used His authority to rebuke the wind and waves: "Quiet! Be still!" Amazingly, the wind died down, and it was completely calm, immediately.

Yes. Jesus has the authority and power over every challenge that tries to stop us from obeying His will and entering into our promises by crossing over. That is why He rebuked the raging storm that was trying to stop them from crossing over. By calming the waves, He showed them that He cared about their well-being, as well as that He has full authority over every storm of life.

Second, use your own authority. The message for the disciples was for them to start using their authority, instead of crying out hopelessly. He told them, another time, the authority they have over nature, if they believe.

He replied, "Because you have so little faith. Truly I tell you, if you have faith as small as a mustard seed, you can say to this mountain, 'Move from here to there,' and it will move. Nothing will be impossible for you."
—Matthew 17:20

NOTHING IS IMPOSSIBLE

Third, cry out to Jesus at any time, and He will respond. The Lord dealt with the disciples' challenges before He corrected them. We witnessed a similar thing when Satan stood before the angel of the Lord to accuse Joshua the high priest. God rebuked Satan before He told the angel to change the garment of the high priest. Therefore, for the Lord to defend His own is the priority. He is our defender. "If anybody does sin, we have an Advocate with the Father—Jesus Christ, the Righteous One" (1 John 2:1).

Fourth, let the Lord deal with your fear. He said to His disciples, "Why are you so afraid? Do you still have no faith?" In this case, He showed them the root cause of their fear was not the storm as much as their doubt and unbelief or lack of faith. The biggest challenge in crossing over is doubt that gives access to fear and unbelief. What we are afraid of is what would stop us from reaching our prophetic destiny and maximizing our God-given potential. The journey of crossing over is to be in God's will, at the right place and at the right time with determination and trust that comes from hearing the Lord. Yes, not only is it impossible to please God without faith, but also it is unthinkable to cross over to reach our prophetic destiny without hearing the clear voice of the Lord, the foundation of our faith and strength for our life's journey to do the will of God. What we hear and believe will either build our faith to overcome challenges or create fear and doubt that will stop us on the way.

The story of Naomi in the Book of Ruth makes this point very clear. Naomi lost everything, and she was in the land of Moab, a place of idol worship. She didn't know how to go back, crossing the wilderness that even the three kings, with all their military power, couldn't cross. But! "When Naomi heard in Moab that the LORD had come to the aid of his people by providing food for them" (Ruth 1:6), Naomi believed the word of the Lord she had heard. Her faith to cross over the massive wilderness to go back to Bethlehem was based on the voice of God. By going back, she corrected what had gone wrong the first time, as well as reentering into the house of bread and provision. Naomi's crossing over to go back also opened the door for Ruth to go forward to enter into the promises of God for future blessings. She became a history maker by becoming part of the genealogy of the Messiah.

Questions for Reflection and Discussion

1. Think back on your journey to a time when you experienced challenges in your pursuit of crossing over. How did you find the courage to move forward, to persevere? And what happened next?

2. Matthew 17:20, quoted in this chapter, is a well-known, beloved text about faith as small as a mustard seed. What does that passage mean to you as you contemplate challenges to crossing over to God's promises?

3. Fear can stop us from reaching our prophetic destiny and maximizing our God-given potential. Contemplate fear in your own life. What may be preventing you from reaching that potential? How might you overcome?

PART FOUR

WHEN HE
Opens . . .

CHAPTER 16

WHEN HE OPENS FOR RELATIONSHIP

I will place on his shoulder the key to the house of David; what he opens no one can shut, and what he shuts no one can open.
—Isaiah 22:22

This prophecy about the coming Messiah is key to establishing the Kingdom of God. The primary call of the Messiah is to open doors for those who will respond to His grace. The first three words in the title of this book are *When He Opens*.

WHEN

The word "when" is about the Lord's timing, which is always perfect. As it is written: "He has made everything beautiful in its time" (Ecclesiastes 3:11). During the earthly ministry of Jesus, people watched the Messiah every day and followed Him to every place He went. They became eyewitnesses to the miracles He performed. The Book of Mark summarizes what they saw: "People were overwhelmed with amazement. 'He has done everything well,' they said. 'He even makes the deaf hear and the mute speak'" (Mark 7:37).

HE

"He" is in reference to the Messiah, the Savior of the world, the Good Shepherd, the King of the universe, the King of kings, and the Lord of lords. The Word Who became flesh and dwelt among us and lived a holy life, Who died for our sins and was risen for our righteousness. He Who has become for us wisdom from God—that is, our righteousness, holiness, and redemption. He was seated at the right hand of the Father with all authority and power on earth and in the heavens. He is the King eternal, immortal, invisible, the only God, Who deserves all honor and glory forever and ever. He created all things for His glory, and in Him all the fullness of God dwells forevermore. He has the Key of David. He is the final authority!

OPENS

The word "opens" refers to His true, absolute, and final authority to open and close. He has the Key of David. This is a picture of the King's final authority, both on earth and in the heavens. He is our Lord and Savior Who says to His children, "I have placed an open door before you that no one can shut." "Opens" also refers to His divine and eternal agenda and purposes. He has loved us and called us for His will and purpose on earth, and He is in us, with us, and for us, to open for us according to His good pleasure and timing. It isn't *if* He will open, but *when* He will open: in His time!

WHEN HE OPENS THE HEAVENS

For us, it is for eternal salvation and relationship as His children. "Open heavens" is a concept of having access into God's presence through Jesus Christ, Who has become our ladder between open heaven and earth. The heavens are where the throne of God is.

The LORD is in his holy temple; the LORD is on his heavenly throne.
—Psalm 11:4

God is the unapproachable light of glory. As human beings, we can only have access into the throne room of God Almighty through Jesus Christ. When Jesus opens the heavens, it is about having access to approach the One Who is on the throne, not just for visitation, but for a lasting transformation. Open heavens are about a divine encounter—a true revelation of Who God is in His holiness, majesty, love, compassion, purity, and more. The experience of the Prophet Isaiah highlights this awesome reality. When the heavens were opened over him, he saw the Lord high and exalted, and he heard the angels calling to one another around Him. They were crying,

"Holy, holy, holy is the LORD Almighty; the whole earth is full of his glory."
—Isaiah 6:3

Because of an extraordinary open heaven, Isaiah saw the glory and heard a voice he had not seen or heard before. This is what happens when the Lord opens the heavens. When He opens, no one can shut its power, and it is guaranteed! Jesus Christ is the only One Who came from the Father to open the heavens that no one can shut. We enter into the presence of the Father through Jesus Christ, Who became the entry point for those who are willing to come through Him to the Father.

"For there is one God and one mediator between God and mankind, the man Christ Jesus, who gave himself as a ransom for all people."
—1 Timothy 2:5–6

GUARANTEED ACCESS TO OPEN HEAVEN, THE THRONE ROOM

When He opens, access is guaranteed forevermore. We can approach the throne of grace anytime with praises and thanksgiving in our hearts. "Let us then approach the throne of grace with confidence, so that we may receive mercy and find grace to help us in our time of need" (Hebrews 4:16).

When He opens heaven, He extends an invitation for us to go up into the throne room. The invitation the Lord Jesus extended to the Apostle John is for every child of God. This door remains open. "Before me was a door standing open in heaven. . . . 'Come up here, and I will show you what must take place after this'" (Revelation 4:1). The call is for us to go higher, for a greater understanding, revelation, and prophetic insight into the future from the throne room perspective. The first opening is for relationship through salvation.

The second opening is forever increasing revelation. "The voice I had first heard speaking to me like a trumpet. . . . At once I was in the Spirit, and there before me was a throne in heaven with someone sitting on it" (Revelation 4:1–2). It is the same voice. He takes us into the throne room for open heavens for a greater revelation. The Apostle Paul also referred to this truth when he gave testimony about His experience in the third heaven. He wrote that he "heard inexpressible things, things that no one is permitted to tell" (2 Corinthians 12:4).

When He opens the heavens, no one is able to shut the access for a relationship, for worship, and an ever-increasing revelation, until we see Him face-to-face.

Questions for Reflection and Discussion

1. Look once again at the graphic contained in this chapter. What stands out to you? What do you notice?
2. How does Isaiah's story in this chapter inspire you?
3. What does the promise that "no one is able to shut the access for a relationship, for worship, for ever-increasing revelation" mean to you? How does that instill hope in your life?

CHAPTER 17

WHEN HE OPENS FOR SPIRITUAL POWER

"I have given you authority to trample on snakes and scorpions and to overcome all the power of the enemy; nothing will harm you."
—Luke 10:19

Being under an open heaven is walking in the kingdom authority the Lord Jesus gave His children to declare the gospel of the Kingdom—for salvation, lasting freedom, and victory. When He opens the heavens to empower His servants, no power on earth is able to stop them. Throughout the Scriptures, whenever the Lord called a person for a special assignment, He gave that individual His power and authority by anointing them for the call. Receiving the anointing was a sign of the presence, approval, power, and authority of God.

Moses gave the command to anoint Aaron as a high priest. "Take the anointing oil and anoint him by pouring it on his head" (Exodus 29:7). That gesture granted God's authority to be on him to serve as the high priest. He received full authority and approval to stand before God, offer sacrifices, pray for the people, instruct people to know and obey God, bless the people in the name of the Lord, and live in the presence of God for God alone. "The high priest, the one among his brothers who has had the anointing oil poured on his head and who has been ordained to wear the priestly garments, must not let his hair become unkempt or tear his clothes . . . nor leave the sanctuary of his God or desecrate it, because he has been dedicated by the anointing oil of his God. I am the Lord" (Leviticus 21:10, 12).

From the day of his anointing, the high priest ministered before God with full power and authority. That was a prophetic picture for the true high priest, Jesus Christ, Who was given all power and authority, both on earth and in the heavens, as He declared: "Then Jesus came to them and said, 'All authority in heaven and on earth has been given to me'" (Matthew 28:18).

The prophets were anointed as a sign of receiving the full authority as they spoke for the Lord. "Also, anoint Jehu son of Nimshi king over Israel, and anoint Elisha son of Shaphat from Abel Meholah to succeed you as prophet" (1 Kings 19:16). That anointing, given to Elisha to minister as the prophet of the Lord, not only was the message from the Lord, but it also brought solutions for society's problems by the prophet's working signs and wonders during his time of ministry. He had the power to heal unhealthful water, answer the questions of kings and ordinary people, raise the dead to life, cleanse lepers, reveal the hindering work of the enemy against the people of the covenant, make flour, and make an axe head float, along with other signs.

In the Old Testament, the kings were anointed to walk with power and authority, to administer justice, and to lead the people of God. King David was the best example of exercising both spiritual and natural authority as a king, not only in leading the people of God, but also in shepherding the people. "And David shepherded them with integrity of heart; with skillful hands he led them" (Psalm 78:72). To do this, King David was sought out and anointed by God Himself. "I have found David my servant; with my sacred oil I have anointed him" (Psalm 89:20).

When the right time came, the Lord confirmed this by sending the prophet Samuel to anoint David among his brothers. "So Samuel took the horn of oil and anointed him in the presence of his brothers, and from that day on the Spirit of the LORD came powerfully upon David" (1 Samuel 16:13). The most important thing in this story is that from that day forward the power of God came upon David to kill Goliath and cast out evil spirits from Saul and set the people of God free from the threat of the enemy to serve God's purposes in his own generation by bringing back the Ark of God, after God's presence had been neglected during King Saul's reign. King David received the divine pattern for Solomon to build the temple of God. All these things were accomplished because of the power and anointing David received.

The anointing and empowerment such as King David had were not limited only to kings whose hearts were after God. God's anointing and empowerment for God's purposes to be fulfilled were also extended to others, even to those who didn't finish well. King Saul is an example. King Saul, the first king who was anointed by Samuel, received both a new heart and the power of the Holy Spirit. After pouring anointing oil upon him Samuel said to Saul, "The Spirit of the LORD will come upon you in power, and you will prophesy with them; and you will be changed into a different person" (1 Samuel 10:6). That is what happened to Saul! He became an extraordinary person, and the power of God came upon him to deliver the people from their enemies. "When Saul heard their words, the Spirit of God came powerfully upon him, and he burned with anger" (1 Samuel 11:6). He started very well by prophesying and bringing deliverance to the nation, but he did not finish well, the way King David did.

KING SAUL'S PARTIAL OBEDIENCE

Saul was the choice of the people. They had asked Samuel to anoint a king for their nation. What Israel failed to realize when they asked for a king to rule over them was this paramount truth: they already had a king, the King of kings. In response, even though His heart was grieved by their request, God granted Saul to be their king. Saul was anointed to lead Israel under God's guidance and instruction, which would come by way of collaboration with Samuel the prophet. It was God's design that together, Saul and Samuel would faithfully carry out His will and purpose for His people (1 Samuel 8, 9). Let's take a look at Saul's life around the time he was anointed king.

Prior to God's appointment of Saul, he was pretty much like any other young man of his time, living and working with his family. On one occasion, his father's donkeys got lost, so he, along with one of his father's servants, was sent out to look for them. After one exhausting search that took them to a distant territory, their hunt yielded no results. The servant suggested they go to the seer—Samuel the prophet—before returning home empty-handed. Saul informed the servant that they had no gift for the prophet, but the servant informed Saul that he did have some money they could give him. So they made their way to the seer.

Prior to Saul's arrival, the Lord let Samuel know that Saul was on his way to see him. Upon Saul's arrival in his town, Samuel welcomed him. To ease Saul's mind, Samuel quickly assured him, through a prophetic word, that his donkeys had been found and he was not to worry about their welfare. Saul had more important matters that he should focus on over the next few days. Samuel invited Saul to spend the night, and the following day he proceeded to give Saul the word of the Lord and anoint him as the king of Israel.

When Samuel delivered the word of the Lord and anointed Saul, he was very specific in his description about the ways in which God would go about confirming this new call. God provided Saul with the confirmation he needed for affirming that call and changed him into a new man by changing his heart. After Samuel's official declaration of Saul as king, the Spirit of the Lord came powerfully upon Saul. From that time forward, He began working through him to deliver His people from their enemies.

A crucial truth must be grasped from this story about Saul: partial obedience is actually total disobedience! Obedience is the hallmark of humility, while disobedience reeks of pride and arrogance.

Following Samuel's confirming message to Saul, he was also very intentional in conveying further instructions. Soon after Saul's anointing ceremony, a group of Philistines assembled to fight Israel. Saul's desire was to offer a sacrifice to the Lord and seek His will in the matter. But Samuel had instructed Saul to wait for him to come so that Samuel, as priest, could perform the sacrifice. The leaders who were not priests knew they were not to offer sacrifices. However, when the king saw that the enemy forces were closing in and that his military was scattering, he panicked. He chose to make the sacrifice himself. He made a major error when he assumed the role of high priest.

As Saul was finishing making the sacrifice, Samuel arrived and asked, "What have you done?" Saul replied, "I thought, 'Now the Philistines will come down against me at Gilgal, and I have not sought the Lord's favor.' So I felt compelled to offer the burnt offering." "You have done a foolish thing," Samuel replied, and he assured Saul his kingdom would not endure (1 Samuel 13:12–13).

Rest assured that as leaders, we will find our character tested along the way in the area of obedience. We will have many opportunities to choose to either move out on our own, as Saul did, or wait upon God. Saul failed to follow Samuel's charge. As a result, he failed to pass a crucial character test.

Anxiety and fear are two of the most common means employed by the adversary to motivate God's people to move outside of His timing. King Saul ended up losing his kingdom because he did not wait on the Lord's timing. Instead, he operated in disobedience.

This issue of timing is very important to the Lord. When a leader fails to recognize and adhere to God's timing in their life, they miss kairos opportunities, the uniqueness of convening under God's providence. Redeeming the time is all about maximizing opportunities through discerning time correctly. Maximized opportunities are the fruit of wisdom.

By asking the question "What have you done?" Samuel was really asking, "How did you become so foolish?" The fear of the Lord is wisdom in its purest sense. When a person walks in the fear of God, it is not as difficult to wait upon His timing.

Again, I stress this fact: our character is most often tested in the area of obedience to the known will of God. Anointing and power without character can't fulfill God's desire. The root of pride, demonstrated by disobedience, can easily be recognized when one rejects higher authority. Saul chose to deny the authority of the one God had placed over him and carried out his own plans, instead of waiting for the high priest. At times, we find it easy to justify our disobedience, but no matter how you slice it, disobedience is disobedience.

Later, the Lord gave Saul a specific assignment to destroy the Amalekites (1 Samuel 15:3). The Amalekites were the first nation to oppose the Israelites' entry into their Promised Land. They refused to let God's people pass through their land and fought against them in attempts to push the nation back into slavery in Egypt. By so doing, they opposed God's will for His chosen people.

Because of the Amalekites' resistance to His plan, the Lord instructed the Israelites through Moses to someday eliminate the Amalekites (Deuteronomy 25:19). Saul was called upon to execute this sentence, and he only partially obeyed. He might as well have ignored the Lord's command completely. The complete testimony is well worth reading (1 Samuel 15).

Saul was given the mandate to attack the Amalekites and totally destroy everything that belonged to them. But Saul and the army spared the Amalekite King Agag and the best of the sheep and cattle, the fat calves, and the lambs. They destroyed what they thought was worthless.

When Samuel learned of Saul's disobedience, he went to confront Saul, who made a dishonest claim: "I have carried out the LORD's instructions." Samuel replied, "Then what is this sound of sheep and cattle I hear?" (1 Samuel 15:14, HCSB).

When Saul opted for partial obedience, he grieved the Lord. As a result of his action, Saul ended up turning away from God. This brings me to my next point. Partial or selective obedience not only is disobedience but also is in all actuality turning against God. The implication of turning away from God means denying His power and authority. Saul demonstrated his disobedience by bringing the Amalekite king back from the battle along with the best cattle. From there, Saul ventured off to build a monument for himself.

In this sad story of a leader called to fulfill God's purpose on earth in his generation, we find a man who did not even show signs of guilt about his disobedience, and he demonstrated no repentance. Instead of going to the temple to offer praise for the victory that God had given to Israel, he traveled to Carmel to build a monument for his own namesake. When a leader's heart turns away from God and personal significance becomes more important than God's purpose and glory, he deceives himself and becomes an idolater of self.

After Saul's compromise—indeed, his disobedience—he even tried to justify his action by saying that he had spared the best of the cattle and oxen for the purpose of sacrificing them to the Lord. A leader's spirituality is not measured by his overt religious activity, but by the purity of his heart, demonstrated through a life of obedience. In God's eyes, to obey is better than sacrifice (1 Samuel 15:22). Creating a religious cover-up while living a life of disobedience quickly leads to a major fall.

The Amalekites represent all that opposes us and the hope and future to which God has called us. God's desire is to destroy everything that attempts to prevent us from entering into our destiny. Our part in His plan of destruction is realized through our obedience to His revealed will. If we do not destroy through our obedience that which opposes us from entering into our purpose, we will be destroyed in the end. What we, as leaders, refuse to destroy will kill us just as it did Saul (2 Samuel 1:6–10).

In the end, Saul's life was taken by an Amalekite. King David, a man after God's heart, commenced his kingdom rulership by killing the Amalekite who had brought about the demise of King Saul, the Lord's anointed.

The concept of sacrifice is important to the Lord, yet He never asks us to do so at the expense of obedience. People's needs are important, but as leaders we are best able to serve others' truest needs as we endeavor to hear and obey the Spirit of the Living God.

Saul chose the fear of people over the fear of the Lord. May we learn well from his example and maintain a posture of wisdom in the fear of the Lord, keeping the main thing: obedience. Humility is forged in the fires of testing that come through obedience to the Lord. May we be a people whose heart's desire is nothing less than complete surrender to His good and perfect will and plan.

When He Opens for Spiritual Power

KING CYRUS AND THE SECRET PLACES

God also called and anointed Cyrus, who didn't know Him, with a plan of revealing Himself in the process of using him to build the temple of God.

> This is what the LORD says to his anointed,
>> to Cyrus, whose right hand I take hold of
>> to subdue nations before him
>> and to strip kings of their armor,
>> to open doors before him
>> so that gates will not be shut:
> I will go before you
>> and will level the mountains;
> I will break down gates of bronze
>> and cut through bars of iron.
> I will give you hidden treasures,
>> riches stored in secret places,
>> so that you may know that I am the LORD,
>> the God of Israel, who summons you by name.
> —Isaiah 45:1–3

In Isaiah 45:1, the Lord promised to activate His power and presence, a sign of true anointing to King Cyrus to rebuild the temple of God. The verse starts with "His anointed." The work of God can't be done without the anointing and power of the Holy Spirit. When Jesus opens the gate that no one can shut, He fills His people with the Holy Spirit to do Kingdom work. As it is written, it is not by might or power but by the Holy Spirit of God. Solomon's temple served as a habitation for the Lord for more than 400 years until King Nebuchadnezzar of Babylon plundered it, taking the gold and silver temple articles and destroying the temple completely by fire. The Jews were taken into captivity and held as slaves for 70 years. It was a hopeless situation until the Lord anointed and raised King Cyrus to defeat Babylon and come to the throne. The prophesied time (Jeremiah 25:11–12) had come for the temple to be rebuilt. King Cyrus was charged by God to allow the Jews to return to Jerusalem if they wished to take part in the rebuilding. He also returned to the Jews all the gold and silver temple articles that Nebuchadnezzar had plundered, so they could be restored to their rightful place in the temple.

Anointing is not limited only to power; it also gives authority. Authority is when God positions us to fulfill His purpose. In other words, authority gives us legal or official permission, or the right to represent the King in His Kingdom. That is walking in divine authority with God. No one shuts the door when we walk with God. Because nothing is impossible for God, He appointed and made a promise to King Cyrus, monarch of Persia, who was anointed by God.

> I will go before you and will level the mountains; I will break down gates of bronze and cut through bars of iron.
> —Isaiah 45:2

The base of authority is a relationship that reflects trust, faith, and wholehearted obedience to the revealed will of God. Open gates also include provision for a person to fulfill the mandate. The provision that the anointing releases isn't limited to financial resources. God's provision in the life of called and anointed people includes spiritual gifts, vision, wisdom, favor, resources, and a pattern for the work to be done. In my book *The King's Signet Ring*, I go into detail about the approval and authority for the Kingdom mandate.

God promised King Cyrus a hidden treasure, even though it might take some time to discover the treasures. "I will give you hidden treasures, riches stored in secret places" (Isaiah 45:3).

The open gate was to have access to the treasure of our Lord, the King of the universe. It was made abundantly clear that the source of all Cyrus's success and accomplishments came from delegated authority from Almighty God. Cyrus accepted the call of God and was used mightily in rebuilding the temple. He finished his assignment. "They finished building the temple according to the command of the God of Israel and the decrees of Cyrus" (Ezra 6:14). When He opens, power, authority, and provision are secured, and God's purpose is done.

When He opens the gates, we have all the access, authority, power, and necessary freedom to live for the glory of the King and advance His Kingdom. That is a life of freedom and victory that no one can shut.

THE DISCIPLES OF JESUS RECEIVED FULL AUTHORITY AND POWER

This was also true for the disciples who were called to ministry in the New Testament. Before He went back to the Father, Jesus told His disciples to stay in Jerusalem until they received the power of the Holy Spirit to go into all the world to make disciples. "I am going to send you what my Father has promised; but stay in the city until you have been clothed with power from on high" (Luke 24:49). After that, he left them and went back to glory and was seated at the right hand of the Father. As the high priest, He entered into the holy of holies. He received full authority to release or clothe His disciples with the power of the Holy Spirit to fulfill their calling under an open heaven. He ascended to heaven, not only to send the Holy Spirit to anoint them, but also to give leaders as ambassadors of His Kingdom. "He who descended is the very one who ascended higher than all the heavens, in order to fill the whole universe. So Christ himself gave the apostles, the prophets, the evangelists, the pastors and teachers" (Ephesians 4:10–11).

Jesus told His disciples to wait until they received the Holy Spirit and power to be His witnesses. The Holy Spirit came upon them like a mighty wind on the Day of Pentecost. The power they received that day became an unstoppable movement for the gospel of salvation. The day the Lord Jesus poured the Holy Spirit upon those who were committed, they received power not only to live for Him and serve His purpose, but also to live and work with Him. The opposition, through over 2,000 years of history, has neither stopped nor shut the door to the gospel of salvation.

Paul gave instructions to be filled with the Holy Spirit (Ephesians 5:18). We are to be controlled and guided by the Holy Spirit to move from glory to glory and from power to power to be more like Him.

When He opens the power, there is a commissioning and sending to advance the Kingdom by using the open door that no one can shut. When He opens doors, opportunities for ministry and for fulfilling His purpose are granted. He opens to reveal His eternal will and pleasure. Open doors are all about the plan and purpose of the remaining days. When a person accepts the call of God wholeheartedly, a person is being set apart to live for God's will. Walking in obedience not only gives us open doors to ministry, but it also gives us open gates to enter into the presence of the King and walk in victory as we do His will. As it is written, "No, in all these things we are more than conquerors through him who loved us" (Romans 8:37.)

It is the King Who gives us open doors and opens the gates. We receive divine approval to become ambassadors of the King of glory to represent the Kingdom. The role of an ambassador in the Kingdom of God starts with anointing. This type of anointing gives a person the delegated authority to act as a representative of the King. It gives authority and approval to be sent. It releases divine power, authority, and provision for the given assignment. In other words, because of the anointing, gate power, authority, and provision are opened for us just as they were for King Cyrus. Hence, the heavenly invitation is this:

> Since we are surrounded by such a great cloud of witnesses, let us throw off everything that hinders and the sin that so easily entangles. And let us run with perseverance the race marked out for us, fixing our eyes on Jesus, the pioneer and perfecter of faith. For the joy set before him he endured the cross, scorning its shame, and sat down at the right hand of the throne of God.
>
> —Hebrews 12:1–2

Questions for Reflection and Discussion

1. What does it mean to "walk in the Kingdom authority" that Christ gave His children?
2. How do the stories of the kings' anointing challenge you for your walk today?
3. How have you experienced God's commissioning and sending to advance the Kingdom?

CHAPTER 18

WHEN HE OPENS FOR UNDERSTANDING

The primary mission of the Lord Jesus is to give us a full understanding of spiritual reality through the gospel of salvation. He came to be the light of the world, and our light, so that we can see and clearly understand the plan and purpose of God. Paul highlights this truth. Everything exposed by the light becomes visible, for it is light that makes everything visible.

> This is why it is said:
> "Wake up, sleeper,
> rise from the dead,
> and Christ will shine on you."
> —Ephesians 5:14

He opened the heavens and came to dwell among us to remove the darkness. "In him was life, and that life was the light of all mankind. The light shines in the darkness, and the darkness has not overcome it" (John 1:3–5).

HE OPENS HEARTS AND MINDS

To have spiritual understanding and revelation in our hearts and minds is key. When the Lord opens our hearts there is repentance, salvation, restoration, and renewal. Through an open heart, a relationship with God is established to receive the Holy Spirit, Who enlightens us. Throughout the Old Testament, God promised a new heart and a renewed spirit.

> I will give you a new heart and put a new spirit in you; I will remove from you your heart of stone and give you a heart of flesh.
> —Ezekiel 36:26

Many other similar verses with signs of hope, restoration, and repentance for salvation are available. God is interested in the heart that is open to His voice to obey Him. The warning in the New Testament is not to harden our hearts when we hear His voice as the Israelites in the wilderness did.

Salvation comes by hearing His voice and responding to it by repenting. When the Lord opens our heart, there is repentance unto salvation. On the Day of Pentecost, when Peter stood and spoke, the first thing the Holy Spirit did was touch hearts. "When the people heard this, they were cut to the heart and said to Peter and the other apostles, 'Brothers, what shall we do?'" (Acts 2:37). Peter told them to repent and be baptized in the name of Jesus Christ. They are the same people who had rejected Jesus until that day. Yes, the Lord opened their hearts, and 3,000 of them gladly repented and received salvation that morning. When He opens a heart, salvation, renewal, and restoration shine the light of His glory. The Lord put the light of His glory in our hearts and told us to shine in the darkness so that those who are blinded by the god of this world will see His light (2 Corinthians 4:4–7). This is why believers are called the light of the world.

Our heart is the source of both life and light. Purity of heart enables us to see God. The Holy Spirit dwells in our hearts. When Paul prayed for the saints in Ephesus, the eyes of their hearts were opened to the hope for wisdom, knowledge, and understanding of the call of God, their rich inheritance, and the surpassing power of the Holy Spirit (Ephesians 1:17–19). This wisdom, knowledge, and understanding released true revelation of the word of God.

When the Lord opens our hearts to see Him, there is the spirit of forgiveness and love. As Stephen was being stoned to death, when he saw God's glory and the Lord Jesus standing at the Father's right hand, he prayed, "Lord, do not hold this sin against them" (Acts 7:60).

When He opens our hearts, we shouldn't have a problem to forgive. When He opens our hearts, we walk not only in forgiveness, but also in true and sincere love.

> The goal of this command is love, which comes from a pure heart and a good conscience and a sincere faith.
> —1 Timothy 1:5

When He opens our hearts, we love Him with all our heart. We love our neighbors as ourselves. We love our enemies and bless those who persecute us. This is transformation to be more like the Lord.

When He opens our minds, we receive wisdom, discernment, understanding, and knowledge, since the Spirit of God rests upon our lives (see Isaiah 11:2).

This type of wisdom and understanding comes from God as the result of God's indwelling presence in us, giving us the mind of Christ. James encouraged us to ask for wisdom from God, Who generously gives when we ask generously. This wisdom makes us not only wise but also effective and productive in what we do.

> The wisdom that comes from heaven is first of all pure; then peace-loving, considerate, submissive, full of mercy and good fruit, impartial and sincere.
> —James 3:17

Wisdom from heaven is what David received to understand the pattern for building the tabernacle. Solomon asked for discernment from God, because his heart was to lead God's people, and God blessed him with great wisdom—more than any of the other kings before him or after him.

The Lord opened the minds of Daniel and his friends. "To these four young men God gave knowledge and understanding of all kinds of literature and learning. And Daniel could understand visions and dreams of all kinds" (Daniel 1:17). In fact, after they passed the test of keeping themselves pure before God in the land of captivity, they became wiser by ten times than others. They glorified the Lord throughout their lives in captivity.

HE OPENS EYES

Jesus is the opener of eyes. He came to open blind eyes. Throughout His ministry, Jesus gave sight to blind people. The people said, "He can even open blind eyes," after Jesus opened the eyes of the man who was born blind, who testified, "I was blind but now I see!" (John 9:25). Jesus opens physical eyes, but even greater is that He opens spiritual eyes. Paul's physical eyes were opened after he had been blinded, but his spiritual eyes were also opened to the truth. When the Lord opens blind eyes, a person sees what he didn't see before. He regains a new perspective in life.

A beautiful story is found in Mark 8:22–25. This man didn't come to Jesus and ask Him to heal his blind eyes, but his friends asked Jesus to heal him. Jesus took him out of the village, spit on his eyes, put His hands on him, and asked if he was seeing anything. The man told Him that he saw people walking around like trees. Distinguishing between people and trees is not only about physical sight issues, but also about value. To correct this, Jesus touched the man's eyes again. At Jesus's second touch, the man's sight and value were both healed completely. Jesus told the man not to go back to the village where he was living as a blind man without hope and a future. When Jesus opens our eyes and minds, we don't want to go back to the old situation that was made hopeless. We go home with a testimony of what God has done.

When the Lord opens our eyes, we receive not only physical eyesight but also spiritual enlightenment. Our vision becomes clear. We see things of the Lord with a new understanding, and this leads us to total obedience to His revealed will. Paul highlighted this when he said very boldly to King Agrippa, "I was not disobedient to the vision from heaven" (Acts 26:19). True vision leads us into a greater determination, as well as a desire to see and honor Him more. David prayed this prayer: "Open my eyes that I may see wonderful things in your law" (Psalm 119:18). We receive revelation of His greatness, majesty, and holiness. The greatest blessing is to see our King and His beauty. This is the promise God has given us as His children: "Your eyes will see the king in his beauty and view a land that stretches afar" (Isaiah 33:17).

HE OPENS EARS

When He opens our ears, we hear His voice. Hearing the voice of God is the greatest blessing we have received from the Lord. Our salvation is the result of our hearing the good news of the gospel. In other words, hearing leads to salvation and eternal life. Without our hearing His word and His voice, there wouldn't be any true repentance. The core of the biblical message is repentance. Repentance is the foundation of salvation, restoration, renewal, awakening, and a return to the plan and purpose of God for life's blessings.

The most important message the Old Testament prophets and the New Testament apostles preached was repentance. God told His people their greatest problem was they didn't hear Him. They refused to hear Him, and they didn't repent and come back to Him. In the New Testament the Lord warns us:

> Today, if you hear his voice,
>   do not harden your hearts
> as you did in the rebellion,
> during the time of testing in the wilderness,
>   where your fathers tested and tried me
> though for forty years they saw what I did.
> —Hebrews 3:7–9

What a warning! The Lord was angry with the people because they refused to hear His voice. Hearing His voice is what separates us from those who don't know Him. Jesus told us that His sheep will hear His voice, they know Him, and they follow Him. The Lord Jesus gave a warning to all seven churches in Revelation chapters 2 and 3: "Whoever has ears, let them hear what the Spirit says to the churches" (Revelation 2:7).

Jesus came to open the heavens over us to establish sonship with us. He opened our ears to hear His voice and then follow. He opened our hearts to welcome Him and our mouths to praise Him and declare His goodness and salvation. He opened our eyes to see Him and follow Him. As He opens the heavens over us, He opens doors of opportunity before us to glorify Him by doing His will on Earth.

Jesus opened for us what sin and the enemy closed. But He declared, as the King of kings and Lord of lords Who rules over us, both for us and for those who came before:

> These are the words of him who is holy and true, who holds the key of David. What he opens no one can shut, and what he shuts no one can open.
> —Revelation 3:7

Questions for Reflection and Discussion

1. As you reflect on your journey of faith thus far, how has God opened your heart and mind and brought about a greater understanding of what it means to live in the light of the Kingdom?

2. When God opens our hearts, we love Him with all our heart. We love our neighbors as ourselves. We love our enemies and bless those who persecute us. In what ways have you seen this promise lived out in your life?

3. How do you respond to the warning from Hebrews 3:7–9 found near the end of this chapter? What from the passage will you tuck in your heart and mind to dwell on further?

CHAPTER 19

WHEN HE OPENS
FOR BLESSINGS

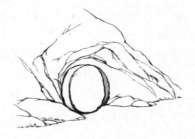

God's plan from the beginning is to bless. We are created in His image and likeness. There is no greater blessing than carrying the image of God and having life as a result of His breathing life into us. He gave human beings dominion over the earth. He made a declaration that it is not good for a man to be alone and gave Adam a companion, Eve, for fellowship. He then blessed them to be fruitful and increase in number—to fill the earth and rule over every living thing He created. That was how mankind started in the beginning—all blessings, including the presence of God. However, because of sin, the curse entered into the world and affected both spiritual blessings and material provision. Jesus came as a second Adam to reverse the curse by paying the price of sin.

> For you know the grace of our Lord Jesus Christ, that though he was rich, yet for your sakes he became poor, so that you through his poverty might become rich.
> —2 Corinthians 8:9

Through His death and resurrection, He opened the heavens for God's blessings through a new covenant relationship for those who believe. "He redeemed us in order that the blessing given to Abraham might come to the Gentiles through Christ Jesus, so that by faith we might receive the promise of the Spirit" (Galatians 3:14).

HE OPENS THE WINDOW OF HEAVEN

Opening the window of heaven is about the blessings God releases upon His covenant people who are faithful in worshiping Him. God promised the Israelites if they returned to Him and honored Him in their tithes, He would open the windows of heaven that no one can shut.

> "Bring the whole tithe into the storehouse, that there may be food in my house. Test me in this," says the LORD Almighty, "and see if I will not throw open the floodgates of heaven and pour out so much blessing that there will not be room enough to store it."
> —Malachi 3:10

The message of this verse is if we honor God by obeying and giving with our tithes, He opens the windows of heaven that will not be shut. Giving is not about meeting needs; God doesn't have a need. But it is about honoring God by recognizing that He is the creator and owner of everything. Giving is part of worshiping God, as well as declaring total dependence upon Him, both for life and daily provision. As this relates to giving, we obey Him through our tithes. That is ten percent of our income.

We also honor Him by our first fruits giving. First fruits giving is about honoring God by making Him first in everything. It is making His Kingdom and His righteousness our priorities. When we put Him first, He adds other things to meet our needs and as special blessings. In other words, if we follow God's guidance, other provisions follow us. By our first fruits, we declare that we will follow Jesus—not seeking material gain or even blessings. Our love gift is to show the compassion and love of God to others. Generosity is God's nature. If we know Who God is and understand that His grace saved us, we become committed to the gospel and decide to live for His glory. Generosity just becomes a part of who we are. I like to call it the 5Gs: God, Grace, Gospel, Glory, and Generosity.

He said that if we obey Him, make Him first, and show His compassion, He opens the windows of heaven to pour down His blessings upon us. He even said, "Test me in this."

When He opens the windows of heaven, the blessings and provisions are to be released in full measure. It is not about meeting needs, but about receiving such blessing that we would not have enough to store it. It is like a floodgate. When God opened the floodgates of heaven, the earth couldn't handle it. It became a destructive force because of the magnitude. When He opens His covenant, blessing is released without measure for the glory of His name. A blessing received from His glory is not only to meet needs but also to show the generosity of God, confirm His covenant and bless us, and make us a blessing in the work of His Kingdom.

HE OPENS PRISON DOORS

Prison is a jail, a place of oppression, a place of constraint, restraint, limitation, restriction, lack of freedom, control, and confinement. Jesus came to bring freedom by setting the prisoners free. A prophecy was spoken about Him, that He would "Proclaim freedom for the captives, and release from darkness for the prisoners" (Isaiah 61:1). Yes, He came to open prison doors for lasting and true freedom from the power of sin. Yes, He Himself said the Son of man has power and the authority to forgive sin. That includes freeing a person from both the results of sin and the power of sin.

So if the Son sets you free, you will be free indeed.
—John 8:36

Jesus broke the power of sin and gave us victory. Death lost its power, and the door of salvation has been opened through Christ Jesus for everyone. Therefore, there is no condemnation for those who are in Christ Jesus. The prison door is opened, and total freedom is declared by the Lord Jesus. Since He opened the door, no one can shut the door to keep individuals in prison without their free will.

This is also true physically as well. Many times, the Lord opened doors for His servants to come out to do His perfect will. Peter was imprisoned and destined to be killed, but the Lord sent His angel and opened the prison door for him to be free again. When Peter was released by the angel of the Lord, prison doors were opened without his effort. "They came to the iron gate leading to the city. It opened to them by itself" (Acts 12:10). Paul and Silas also had a very similar, but more dramatic experience in prison. They were worshiping at midnight, and quickly everything changed. "Suddenly there was such a violent earthquake that the foundations of the prison were shaken. At once all the prison doors flew open, and everyone's chains came loose" (Acts 16:26).

In this sense, prison is what takes away our freedom to hold us back from the plan and purpose of God. The One Who came to proclaim freedom for the prisoners and set the oppressed free through His death and resurrection has opened all the prison doors. If you are in any kind of bondage, captivity, or oppression, call upon His name. Calling upon His name is all that is required. He opens doors for you, and you enjoy true freedom forevermore. When He opens, no prison door can hold us back. Yes, He has the Key of David. What He opens, no one can shut!

HE OPENS WOMBS

When He opens, barren wombs become a fruitful, productive place. When He opens, desolation is broken and productivity is released in individuals' lives, over cities, peoples, and nations. Barren land becomes a fruitful place when He opens. Yes, He is the creator, and He is also the restorer.

> The desert and the parched land will be glad; the wilderness will rejoice and blossom.
> —Isaiah 35:1

When He opens, nothing remains unproductive or fruitless and wasted. He opens so we will have fruitfulness in everything we do.

When He opens a barren woman, she gives birth, supernaturally. Barren women become mothers of children. There are a number of examples of this throughout the Bible. To mention a few, let us start with Sarah. God promised Abraham to multiply his descendants and bless nations through his seed. However, Abraham and Sarah were advanced in age and had no child. The Lord had not allowed Sarah to have a child, so out of desperation, she gave Abraham her servant girl, Hagar, to sleep with. He did as she suggested, without asking God. Although Hagar got pregnant and had a son, Ishmael, their plan didn't work. God's plan was for Sarah to have a child. In due time, in the timing of the Lord, the Lord remembered Sarah. Because of age, Sarah's womb was dead, and Abraham's body was also as good as dead; however, he believed God without weakening in faith. Since God opens what no one can shut, not even old age or nature can stop Him; He came through for them by opening Sarah's womb. "Now the LORD was gracious to Sarah as he had said, and the LORD did for Sarah what he had promised. Sarah became pregnant and bore a son to Abraham in his old age, at the very time God had promised him" (Genesis 21:1–2).

Over the years, I have personally prayed for couples who were told by doctors they could not have children. But the Lord opened their wombs and blessed them with children. I have dedicated a number of them to the Lord. (I recognize that some readers may have prayed for a barren womb to be blessed with children, and that has not yet happened.) A few years ago, I was ministering at a conference in Israel. At the conclusion of my message, I was prompted by Holy Spirit to pray for a few individuals as directed by the Lord. I called out to a woman sitting on the second row. She came forward. I had never seen her before. As I was getting ready to pray for her, ushers came to stand behind her. I looked up and saw a person who was sitting in another row. I called him out and told him to stand behind her as catcher. I asked the ushers to move away. I prayed a simple prayer for the fire of God to enter into the woman's womb. She was touched by the Holy Spirit's power. After two years, I went back to Israel to minister at another gathering. At the end of the ministry, a couple came forward with a beautiful little girl. They gave me warm greetings with big smiles on their faces. They commented that I didn't know them, and I wasn't remembering them. They were right!

They said about two years earlier I had called her to the front. Before I prayed, I had called the man from the back to catch her. It was her husband, but I didn't realize it. Before they came for the conference, the doctor had told them there was no hope of their having a child. They had tried for 11 years. The fact that

I called the woman and her husband to come forward without knowing who they were was amazing. Praying for the fire of God to enter into her stomach completely surprised them. They went home filled with faith and hope. They conceived the same month. "We brought her today," they said, "for you to honor us by dedicating our baby daughter to the Lord." This is only one testimony, but I have heard so many similar testimonies. Last year, my wife and I went to Brazil to speak at a conference. During the three-day conference, five different families came up to us with their children to give testimonies. I have pictures with many of them, but I have not asked their permission to publish them.

Yes, He opens barren wombs!

The story of Hannah is very similar. She cried for a child for many years without any answer. In her hopelessness, she went to the temple to pour out her heart before the Lord. Even though she was misunderstood by Eli, the high priest, the Lord heard her prayer, and she gave birth to Samuel, the prophet, judge, and priest, who held three offices, just like the Lord Jesus. He became the true prophet of all Israel and was known as the appointed prophet of the Lord, whose word was fulfilled without failing. The Lord opened Hannah's womb. When He opened, Isaac and Samuel were born.

The story about Elizabeth and Zechariah is another miracle story. They served the Lord all their lives and lived righteously in the sight of God, and they were blameless, but without children. "They were childless, because Elizabeth was not able to conceive; and they were both very old" (Luke 1:7). That was until the angel came with the good news that Elizabeth would give birth to a son, and his name would be John. Even though she had a hard time believing John would be born, John became the forerunner to prepare the way for Jesus. When He opens, no womb remains barren.

HE OPENS GRAVES

Resurrection is a second chance. Jesus said, "I am the resurrection and the life." That means our God is the God of again—a second chance for individuals, families, ministries, businesses, and life in general. What is lost can be found! What is dead lives again. What is buried rises again. Lost hope is restored.

> Prophesy and say to them: "This is what the Sovereign LORD says: 'My people, I am going to open your graves and bring you up from them; I will bring you back to the land of Israel.'"
> —Ezekiel 37:12

Dry and scattered bones gather again and experience life in its fullness. Hope is restored. Graves open and give up the dead. Hopeless dry bones become a mighty army of the Lord for victory when He opens graves. Discouragement changes into great hope. Darkness changes into a bright light of hope and possibilities. The Israelites lost hope, and they believed it would be impossible to have a future and hope as a nation.

> Our bones are dried up and our hope is gone; we are cut off.
> —Ezekiel 37:11

But that was until the Lord came, opened their graves, and affirmed to them His plan of a future and prosperity.

Graves and tombs are signs of hopelessness, desperation, and the end of everything. But our God is a God of resurrection and life! Reality is in the story of Lazarus's death, very clearly. Mary and Martha sent a message to Jesus, asking Him to come and heal their sick brother before it would be too late. Jesus told the messengers that this sickness was not for death, but for God's glory, and he stayed two more days where he was.

They lost hope when Lazarus died and they buried him. When Jesus came, Lazarus had been four days in the tomb. Jesus told them to open the grave by removing the stone. But the sisters responded by telling Him it was too late. At this point Jesus responded:

> Did I not tell you that if you believe, you will see the glory of God?
> —John 11:40

First, they should have believed the word of Jesus. It is for the glory of God. The only way to see the glory of God in a hopeless situation is by believing and standing on God's Word. Second, they should have believed that His time is always right. Third, they should have believed that He is the resurrection and the life. Fourth, they should have believed He is able to call out that which is dead as though it were alive. This is precisely what Jesus did. He asked where they had buried Lazarus, and He stood in front of the tomb and called out Lazarus with a loud voice. Lazarus came out with grave clothes on, and Jesus told them to untie him and let him go.

Yes, when He opens the grave, the dead rise and hope is restored. Not only the Lord Jesus but also the apostles raised the dead in the power of the name of Jesus. Our grave was opened the day we accepted the Lord Jesus as our personal Savior. We crossed over from death to life at that very moment. We received resurrection life and eternal life.

> When the perishable has been clothed with the imperishable, and the mortal with immortality, then the saying that is written will come true: "Death has been swallowed up in victory."

"Where, O death, is your victory?
Where, O death, is your sting?"
—1 Corinthians 15:54–55

The greatest blessing is the hope of His coming, which is the completion of our blessings, "While we wait for the blessed hope—the appearing of the glory of our great God and Savior, Jesus Christ" (Titus 2:13). Finally, when He opens the heavens to invite us into eternal joy, He is saying:

"Then the King will say to those on his right, 'Enter, you who are blessed by my Father! Take what's coming to you in this kingdom. It's been ready for you since the world's foundation.'"
—Matthew 25:34 MSG

Questions for Reflection and Discussion

1. What has your concept of "blessing" been prior to reading this chapter? How has it changed?
2. Which of the "openings" in this chapter (heaven, prison, wombs, graves) strikes you the most deeply? Why might that be?
3. What encouragement do you derive from the knowledge that Christ will open the grave, and the dead will rise and hope will be restored?

CONCLUSION

As we have seen throughout this book, the concept of open heavens is a desire for God's presence among His people to protect, guide, provide, and create genuine, tangible signs of His presence through His act of mercy and grace. Closed heavens are about God's judgment, while open heavens signify His mercy and compassion.

The first family, Adam and Eve, started under an open heaven with God. But because of sin, they were put out, not only of the garden of Eden but also from fellowship with God. The closing of the garden was also a picture of the heavens closing. This is what resulted in curses, rather than blessings. Since that time, the desire of every sincere follower of God is to have the same kind of fellowship with God, under an open heaven.

Open heavens are about the manifested presence of God in the context of our relationship with Him. They are about knowing Him, establishing our personal identity, and affirming our prophetic destiny to fulfill our divine purpose on Earth because of our relationship with the God of an everlasting covenant. The concept of open heavens can't be a reality without understanding and walking in a covenant relationship, since it's a restoration of divine presence and the Lord's goodness. In a covenant, God opens the heavens over us, while He opens doors before us, so that as His children, we can open the gates of our lives, ministries, cities, and nations for establishing His Kingdom authority! (See Psalm 24:7–10). Yes, open heavens affirm covenantal relationship for a greater, deeper revelation that leads to true restoration for lasting transformation in every dimension of our lives.

However, in order for us to first develop our spiritual life, we need to have a covenantal relationship with the Lord. Jesus opened the heavens and came to give us access to the Father. He became the only entry point to have an eternal relationship with God. He referred to Himself as the only true door that no one can shut, for those who would like to come to the Father through Him. That is why He said, "I am the door; by me if any man enters in, he shall be saved, and shall go in and go out, and shall find pasture" (John 10:9, ASV).

We are born again when we open our hearts to the Lord and we invite Him in as our Lord and Savior without restriction. This opening of our heart also means a willingness to invite Him into our lives. It shows our availability to follow Him all the way with all our heart, to live for His purpose, and to do His will on Earth. We are a new creation because of the new relationship with Him. Our spiritual journey begins by coming to the Father through Jesus Christ, Who is the true door. The sign of our willingness to go through the open door, Jesus, is to open our lives and invite Him in to dwell with us by the person of the Holy Spirit. He knocks at the door of every person's heart for a new beginning. When a person opens his heart to the Lord, the Lord opens the door of salvation for an eternal relationship. This individual is called to become a new creation. At that time, the Lord also opens the heavens to a person to be seated on the throne with Him (Ephesians 2:6), and to enjoy all spiritual blessings in Jesus Christ in heavenly realms.

The desire and prayer of the Prophet Isaiah was, "Oh, that you would rend the heavens and come down, that the mountains would tremble before you!" (Isaiah 64:1). Yes, the heavens were opened, and the curse was broken. The good news of salvation was declared by the angels on the day the Word became flesh in the tabernacle among us. Open heavens over us mean a divine invitation to start a lasting relationship by opening our hearts for Him to come and dwell in us and with us. They also mean to establish His Kingly authority in our lives and on earth through us. This gives us not only authority but also responsibility to open the gates as a trusted servant for the King of Glory to come in and into our spheres of influence. This is called opening the gate for the King of Glory.

When we open our heart to the Lord, He opens the heavens over us by removing all the curses of sin and inequity for our blessing of having a lasting relationship with Him. That gives the authority and the key to open the gates for Him to come in. As the result of our ongoing relationship with Him as children, He gives us open doors to do His will on earth in obedience to His voice.

As we have seen in the pages of this book, opening and closing doors, gates, and the heavens are very important. These three concepts have been mentioned throughout the Bible. Understanding their relationship and balancing them is the key to our relationship to Him, as well as establishing our prophetic destiny and understanding our role in Kingdom work.

- Open heavens are a divine invitation for a relationship with Him for covenant and intimacy.
- Open doors are a divine invitation for our destiny to live a life of obedience, to run the race faithfully, and to be fruitful for the glory of God.
- Open gates are a divine invitation for the Kingdom mandate to honor Him, as we prepare the way for the full manifestation for the nations to see and honor the King of Glory, Who is coming soon.
- Open windows are a divine invitation to receive His blessings through a life of obedience.

When He opens the heavens over us for a true and lasting relationship that is being established, fellowship is affirmed. A true identity is being realized for God's blessings to be released and for His approval to be declared. When He opens doors, the calling is realized and a true commission for the purpose of God is affirmed to do His will and fulfill His purpose on earth. The bridge between the heavens and earth becomes tangible, and the Lord's prayer is answered. "Let your will be done on earth as it is in heaven." This gives Kingdom workers the keys of the Kingdom to open the gate for the King of Glory to come in, as well as to receive the authority to speak to the ancient gates to open up. "Lift up your heads, you gates; be lifted up, you ancient doors, that the King of glory may come in" (Psalm 24:7). He comes in to reign and rule. This is the proclamation of Revelation 11:15, spoken with loud voices in heaven:

> The Kingdom of the world has become the Kingdom of our Lord and of his Messiah, and he will reign for ever and ever.

Open heavens over you are a divine invitation (Revelation 4:1), not only for a new relationship, but for a lasting relationship, while open doors represent the opportunities He provides to be fruitful, walking in obedience and by faith to fulfill our calling. The core of our calling and prophetic destiny to declare the glory of King Jesus on Earth is to open the gates and introduce Him as the King of kings and Lord of lords—the Savior of the world.

As we have studied these interrelated concepts of openings and closings, let us make a firm decision.

- First, stay under open heavens by protecting your ongoing relationship and responding to the heavenly invitation, "Come up here" (Revelation 4:1).
- Second, receive the power of the Holy Spirit and the revelation of His Word to know and walk through open doors that He places before you every day in spirit obedience and sincere faith (Revelation 3:7–8).

- Third, know your values with a biblically based belief system, establish your identity and commit to your purpose. In the Kingdom of God these make us a VIP (an individual with value, identity, and purpose), creating a difference in our generation by serving His purpose and impacting our generation for the glory of God.

Our decision is also born out of a deep reflection on biblical narratives on open heavens, open doors, open gates, and open hearts that embrace the spiritual power of a life in Christ. Throughout this book God has been inviting you to embrace in obedience your divine invitation from Him to walk through the doors He opens and to fulfill your calling by opening the gates for the King of Glory, the Lord Jesus Christ.

Are you willing to allow Him to open doors, gates, and the heavens in your life? Do you understand all that He has done in preparing the heavens to be opened for you during certain seasons and times in your life? Make a decision to accept all that He has prepared for you through His Word and the prophetic direction that has been established for you. Increase your relationship with the Lord, so you will be positioned to receive every good and perfect gift He has already given you through every open door, every open gate, and every open heaven. Walk in the authority that comes with an open heaven. Your life will be changed forever for the glory of God!

A NOTE ON TERMS

Throughout this book, you will find several terms with which you may be unfamiliar. To help you make the most of the book, here are brief definitions or contexts for those terms:

1. OPEN HEAVENS—Throughout the Old Testament, God spoke to the Israelites about an open heaven. An open heaven provided the miraculous provision of their daily manna while they were wandering in the wilderness for 40 years. In Psalm 78:23–24, we read, "Yet he gave a command to the skies above and opened the doors of the heavens; he rained down manna for the people to eat, he gave them the grain of heaven." An open heaven was a supernatural sign from God of provision. Deuteronomy 28:12 records, "The Lord will open the heavens, the storehouse of his bounty, to send rain on your land in season and to bless all the work of your hands." Malachi 3:10 states, "'Bring the whole tithe into the storehouse, so that there may be food in My house, and test Me now in this,' says the Lord of hosts, 'and see if I will not open the floodgates of heaven and pour out so much blessing that there will not be room enough to store it.'" This promise of an open heaven was not only addressed in the Old Testament, but it continued in the New Testament as well.

    John 1:51 states, "He then added, 'Very truly I tell you, you will see "heaven open, and the angels of God ascending and descending on" the Son of Man.'" Acts 7:56 says, "'Look,' he said, 'I see heaven open and the Son of Man standing at the right hand of God.'" Acts 10:11 declares, "He saw heaven opened and something like a large sheet being let down to earth by its four corners." Israel had to learn how to live by faith under an open heaven, and so do we.

2. CLOSED HEAVENS—A closed heaven is when there is a barrier between heaven and earth, when there is no longer the ability to hear the voice of God, which occurs many times because of the presence of sin. First Kings 8:35 says, "When the heavens are shut

up and there is no rain because your people have sinned against you, and when they pray toward this place and give praise to your name and turn from their sin because you have afflicted them . . ." The difference between an open and a closed heaven is when mankind chooses to close off the voice of God—the revelation or supernatural wisdom that only comes through the Holy Spirit.

3. TABERNACLE—The tabernacle of Moses was the temporary place of worship that the Israelites built according to God's specifications while wandering in the wilderness. They used it until King Solomon built the temple. The word *tabernacle* is a translation of the Hebrew word *mishkan*, which means "dwelling place." The tabernacle of Moses followed traditional structures and consisted of an outer court, an inner court, and the Holy of Holies (Exodus 27:9–19). The purpose of Moses's tabernacle was to provide a place where the people could properly worship God. Priests sacrificed animals on the altar in the outer court. The bread of the presence, the continually burning lampstand, and the offering of incense were all in the Holy Place. Once a year, the high priest would enter the Holy of Holies as part of the ceremony of the Day of Atonement (Leviticus 16). At no other time was anyone to enter the Holy of Holies, as the presence of God dwelt with the Ark of the Covenant.

When Jesus was crucified, the veil between the Holy Place and the Holy of Holies in the temple was torn from the top to the bottom, representing that sin could no longer keep us separated from God (Matthew 27:51). Through His sacrifice on the cross, the Lord fulfilled for all time the requirements for us to be ushered back into the presence of God, where the Scripture says, "Let us therefore come boldly to the throne of grace, that we may obtain mercy and find grace to help in time of need" (Hebrews 4:16, NKJV).

4. OPEN DOORS—When the Bible refers to open doors, whether on earth or in heaven, it is simply implying that God is supernaturally making a way for His work and service to be accomplished. Revelation 4:1 says, "After these things I looked, and behold, a door *standing* open in heaven! And the first voice which I heard like *the sound* of a trumpet speaking with me, saying, 'Come up

here, and I will show you what must take place after these things'" (NASB). Revelation 3:8 declares, "I know your deeds. See, I have placed before you an open door that no one can shut. I know that you have little strength, yet you have kept my word and have not denied my name." In Colossians 4:3, the Apostle Paul states, "And pray for us, too, that God may open a door for our message, so that we may proclaim the mystery of Christ, for which I am in chains." And in 1 Corinthians 16:8–9, Paul says, "But I will stay on at Ephesus until Pentecost, for a great door for effective work has opened to me, and there are many who oppose me."

5. OPEN GATES—Second Peter 1:11 says, "And God will open wide the gates of heaven for you to enter into the eternal kingdom of our Lord and Savior Jesus Christ" (NIV 1984). Again, whether it's physically on earth or it's supernatural, God has a way of opening and closing the areas or gates He wants closed in our lives. Isaiah 45:1 states, "This is what the LORD says to his anointed, to Cyrus, whose right hand I take hold of to subdue nations before him and to strip kings of their armor, to open doors before him so that gates will not be shut. . . ."

6. Ephesians 4:11–13 give us the ministry of the fivefold—"So Christ himself gave *the apostles, the prophets, the evangelists, the pastors* and *teachers*, to equip his people for works of service, so that the body of Christ may be built up until we all reach unity in the faith and in the knowledge of the Son of God and become mature, attaining to the whole measure of the fullness of Christ."
    Apostle—A strategic leader to build a biblical foundation
    Prophet—A visionary leader to provide direction and
        correction
    Evangelist—A motivator and relationship builder to
        advance the cause
    Pastor—A shepherd to protect and manage the flock
        (people)
    Teacher—A trainer and coach to build the capacity for
        the maturity of character and effectiveness.

7. PROMISED LAND—In the Bible, the term "Promised Land" refers to a geographic piece of land that God set aside for His chosen people—the offspring of Abraham (Genesis 12, Genesis 26:3, Genesis 28:13, Numbers 34:1–12). God first gave this pledge of land to Abraham saying, "I will establish your borders from the Red Sea to the Mediterranean Sea, and from the desert to the Euphrates River" (Exodus 23:31). The Israelites didn't begin to move toward the Promised Land until after 400 years of slavery, when Moses delivered them out of Pharaoh's hands. However, they still weren't ready to receive what God had prepared for them because of their fear of the giants who were living there, and as a result, they wandered in the wilderness for another 40 years until Moses left and put Joshua in charge. Joshua and Caleb were the only two, out of the ten spies, who were initially ready 40 years earlier to "go in and take the land." God honored their faith, and they led the people in to finally claim the land that God had promised them.

It's my hope that having this background as you enter the text will aid you as you read and make applications to your life.

SCRIPTURE CREDITS

ACKNOWLEDGMENTS

The first and most important One I would like to acknowledge and thank personally is the Lord Jesus Christ. My life would not be what it is if You had not chosen me and called me to do Your work. Your love and constant presence have made my life immensely rewarding. It has been such an honor to serve You and the body of Christ with the wisdom and prophetic depth you have revealed to me over the years—both in my speaking engagements and in the many books you've had me write. I love You, and I am so grateful You love me, and You have always had great plans for my life. I so look forward to all You have for me, because I know my latter days will be even better than my former days.

I would also like to acknowledge and thank my wife, Genet, and my family for all the sacrifices you have been willing to make for me to follow God's plan for my life. Your love and support have helped me minister the Word of God to believers and unbelievers from all over the globe. Words cannot express my gratitude for God's blessing me with such a wonderful family.

ABOUT THE AUTHOR

Dr. Alemu Beeftu, founder and president of Gospel of Glory, has a heart for training pastors, businessmen, and politicians with a goal of building national leadership infrastructures. Dr. Beeftu presently concentrates on transformational leaders of various ages in more than 54 countries who have the calling, gifting, and character to foster sustainable societal change for the Kingdom of God.

Dr. Beeftu earned a BA from Biola University and master's and doctoral degrees in Curriculum Design and Community Development from Michigan State University. More than 35 years of practice in these and related fields have made Dr. Beeftu an accomplished and sought-after leadership trainer. He also continues to provide leadership worldwide for the Body of Christ.

Dr. Beeftu's most recently authored books include these: *Abiding In His Presence, Rekindle the Altar Fire, The King's Signet Ring, Breakout for Breakthrough, Divine Pattern for the Fullness of His Glory, God's Questions, Restoration for Lasting Transformation, Wrestling for Your Prophetic Destiny, Put Your Heart Above Your Head, Restoring the Altar for Fresh Fire, Leadership Journey, Spiritual Accountability, Leading for Kingdom Impact, Determination to Make a Difference,* and others.

Dr. Beeftu and his wife, Genet, make their home in Highland Village, Texas, with their children, Keah and Amman.

To obtain more information about Dr. Beeftu and how to invite him to speak to your organization, visit www.goglory.org or send an email. Email: gog@goglory.org

Mailing address:
P.O. Box 1719
Lake Dallas, TX 75065

ABOUT PARACLETE PRESS

PARACLETE PRESS IS THE PUBLISHING ARM of the Cape Cod Benedictine community, the Community of Jesus. Presenting a full expression of Christian belief and practice, we reflect the ecumenical charism of the Community and its dedication to sacred music, the fine arts, and the written word.

Learn more about us at our website:
www.paracletepress.com
or phone us toll-free at 1.800.451.5006

SCAN
TO
READ
MORE

More from Paraclete Press

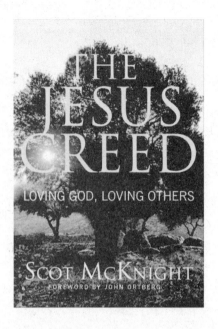

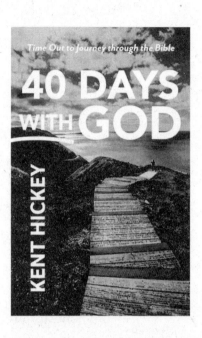

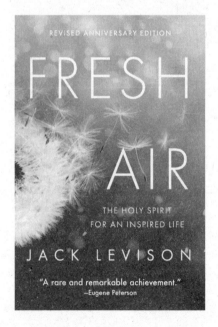

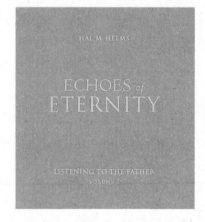